Adam's Belle

A Memoir of Love Without Bounds

To Daryl Scott
Thank you for your support Best
wishes.

Joyce Burnett

February 26, 2011

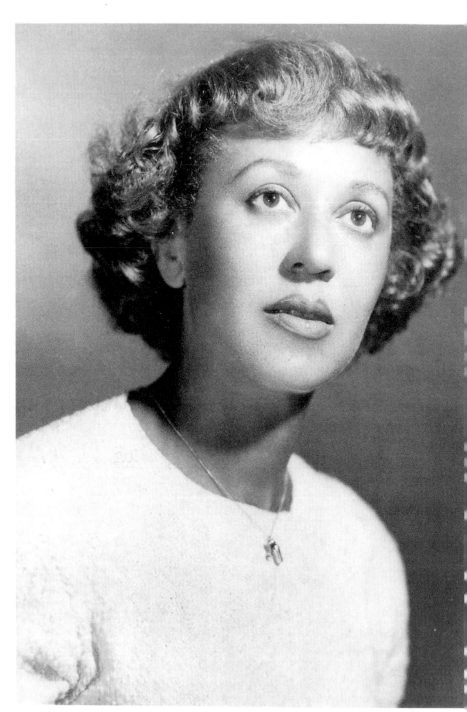

Isabel Washington Powell – 1930's

Adam's Belle

A Memoir of Love Without Bounds

by
Isabel Washington Powell

with
Joyce Burnett

DBM Press, LC
Springfield, VA
2008

First published in 2008 by

DBM Press, LC
6412 Brandon Ave, #123
Springfield, VA 22150
dbmpress@yahoo.com

See our catalogue at http://www.dbmpress.com

For quality used and rare books, see our catalogues at:
 http://www.dbookmahn.com

Library of Congress Control Number:2008927586

ISBN-10 0-9816102-1-8
ISBN-13 978-0-9816102-1-4

Printed in the United States of America

First Edition
1st Printing

1 2 3 4 5 6 7 8 9 10

Produced for the publisher by
BRIOprint, 12 S. Sixth Street, #1020, Minneapolis, MN 55402

DUST JACKET DESIGNED BY DBM PRESS, LC

Contents

Dedication

Isabel dedicates this book to the men in her life
- Adam, Preston, and Tommy

This book is also dedicated to Loice M. Swafford, the best mother in the world. Even though you taught us about the love of Jesus Christ, I still don't understand how you raised nine children without killing any of us. Thank you for showing me that the best is yet to come.

Thank you Isabel for teaching me that we must remember and record the past so that we can place the present and future in the proper context.

Acknowledgements

This book would not have been possible without the help and support of so many people. A special thanks to Brenda Johnson and Evelyn Horad. It was because of them that I learned about this project and met Isabel. Thank you to Tania Padgett who has been on board from the very beginning. Thank you to all the people who granted me interviews including the late Maude Russell and Rosebud Washington, Isabel's younger sister. Thank you also to Wil Haygood for your assistance and permission to use the pictures. A general thank you to the Washington family and friends, whose cooperation enabled this project to come into existence. Many thanks to John Taylor across the ocean, you rock! A special thank you to the Amistad Research Center at Tulane University, for permission to use the Isabel Washington Powell Papers. A very special thank you to Bill and to my sisters Barbara, Katrina, and LaVern, who have always been there for me. Thank you also to Joan Jerry for your words of wisdom and encouragement.

Introduction

Isabel Washington Powell's story is an extraordinary one – born into relative poverty in the deep south in the first decade of the twentieth century, losing her mother at a tender age, and sent away to school, she might have lived and died in obscurity, but the beautiful and spirited Isabel Washington was not born to live a forgettable life. Possessed by a dream, and remarkable confidence in herself, she ran away from home at the age of sixteen "to do something big, to go on the stage and live high." Against all odds, she, and her beloved older sister Fredi, did just that. Fredi was the first to taste the limelight of a theatrical career. In 1922, reasonably content with her bookkeeping job at Black Swan records, Fredi Washington was lured by the prospect of doubling her income into auditioning for the Broadway hit *Shuffle Along*, composed by the legendary Eubie Blake and Noble Sissle, with a book by Flournoy Miller and Aubrey Lyles, and starring the brilliant Florence Mills. In *Shuffle Along's* "Happy Honeysuckle" chorus Fredi worked with the soon-to-be-legends Josephine Baker and Paul Robeson, and learned the skills that gave her a ten-year dancing career.

In "Adam's Belle," Isabel recalls her desire to follow Fredi into show business, reporting that she made her first record in 1923, at the age of fifteen, and joined the cast of *Runnin' Wild*, another Miller and Lyles hit, in September 1924. Isabel and her sister Fredi also performed at the popular nightclubs The Cotton Club, where they danced to orchestrations by Fletcher Henderson, Duke Ellington and Cab Callaway, and Connie's Inn, a favorite of heiress A'lelia Walker.

In the next five years, Isabel endured an early, troubled marriage, the constant shifts in balancing motherhood with work, and the loss of her first husband. Undaunted, she returned to the stage in 1929, winning considerable attention as the "riotous Cordelia" in Wallace Thurman's *Harlem*. In June of 1929, Isabel won even more admiration for her standout performance in the musical comedy *Bomboola*. Moreover the New York Times critic recommended that the creators revise the show to accommodate her talent. That same year, Isabel made her film debut, in *St. Louis Blues*, starring the celebrated Bessie Smith, and also performed on Harlem stages, appearing in three brief comedies at the Alhambra Theatre in 1928: *Market Day, Jazz Holiday,* and *The Beauty Parlor.* In 1931, Isabel appeared with her sister Fredi in *Singin' the Blues*, a musical melodrama of Harlem nightlife, featuring Eubie Blake's orchestra, Frank Wilson as an inadvertent murderer eluding the police, Isabel as his self-sacrificing sweetheart, and Fredi as the bad girl, variously described as a "Harlem trull," a "Lenox Avenue gold digger," and an "evil intrigante." The sister act created a sensation, their distinctive personal styles offering audiences a striking contrast: Isabel, with a head of unruly curls, was hot; Fredi, sleekly bobbed, was cool; Isabel was sexy; Fredi was suave.

After seeing Isabel's performance, Florence Ziegfeld offered her the role of Julie in the first revival of *Showboat.* Her star was rising, but romance intervened. By this time Isabel had met the love of her life, Adam Clayton Powell, Jr., then the charismatic heir apparent to Harlem's largest Baptist congregation, destined to become the first black congressman from the state of New York and a militant activist for civil rights. "Show business" was hardly an appropriate occupation for the wife of the minister of Harlem's largest congregation, so Isabel abandoned her career, and they married in 1933. Sister Fredi found love at precisely the same time, marrying Ellington trombonist Lawrence Brown (also the son of a Baptist minister) that same year. Fredi and Brown, however, continued their performing careers, and Fredi's fame mounted with her performances in the films *The Emperor Jones* and *Imitation of Life*, as well as stage appearances in *Run Little Chillun!* and *Mamba's Daughters.* Just as romance flowered for the sisters simultaneously, so it withered. In 1945, Powell asked Isabel for a divorce to wed twenty-three year old Hazel Scott, also a musical performer. In 1947 Fredi Washington and Lawrence Brown separated because of his numerous infidelities and somewhat open affair with Ellington vocalist Kay Davis. Fredi and Brown divorced in 1951, and she remarried a year later.

For Isabel, though, there would be no replacing Adam. The end of her marriage seems to have been a bolt from the blue. In *Adam's Belle*, she recalls her reaction to Powell's announcement that he is leaving her as one of stunned disbelief. Given the circumstances, the joy and magnanimity with which she recalls their relationship is remarkable. There must have been a horde of men who would have liked to console the still-radiant Isabel, but no one could compete with her "Bunny." She lived a relatively quiet life after her divorce, teaching, and appearing as herself in several documentaries including *Brown Sugar* (1986) and *Keep the Faith, Baby* (2002). Adam's Belle is a remarkable documentation of a fascinating and triumphant American life. Joyce Burnett has provided us with a rare firsthand account of what it was like to live as a black woman with big dreams in the twentieth century, faithfully capturing Isabel Washington's words and her indomitable spirit. Isabel Washington dreamed of a theatrical career, and she achieved it, only to surrender it, apparently with no regrets, for a greater dream of love and personal happiness. When that ended, she took comfort from her family and friends and a new career to keep her energetically engaged in living for another six decades. Bereft of bitterness, self-pity, or regret, Isabel Washington Powell's story astonishes as it inspires. I am grateful to Joyce Burnett for setting it down and sharing it with the rest of us.

Dr. Cheryl Black
Associate Professor and Director of Graduate Studies
Department of Theatre,
University of Missouri
Columbia, MO

CHAPTER 1

Big Momma and the Peanut Man

Early Sunday morning, when the alarm rang out, I rolled over and tried to play sleep – only the alarm was the voice of Big Momma who was as determined as a drill sergeant to get me up. It was God's day and she was in no mood to take any mess. When I heard my tiny body say I was too tired to get up and go to church, Big Momma's voice shook me like a small earthquake. Playing all day, eating food that she cooked and paid for, and causing havoc everywhere I went, left no reason to be tired. I had better get up if I didn't want her to tap my little fanny. Oh, and if I got up right now, this instant, there might be time to roll out the dough. I jumped out of bed.

Big Momma, my maternal grandmother, is the one who raised us. Her real name was Ella Brown. Like many a Southern grandmother in Savannah, Georgia, she ruled her family with an iron fist and with as much love as you could pour into a homemade peach cobbler. I was usually the last one up in the house and even though I know I gave her much grief on a daily basis, I knew better than to really mess with Big Momma. Respecting your elders was the number one rule to Big Momma. She never gave up on anyone in the household, least of all me.

Big Momma lived on the other side of town. She helped take care of my great grandfather and his wife who lived with her until they passed away. My great grandfather made caskets; back then they were usually just pine boxes. The idea of Big Momma having parents was kind of funny to me. She seemed to be in charge of everything and everybody. I couldn't imagine anyone ruling over her. We saw Big Momma so much that it felt like she lived at our house. We had a typical Southern three-story walk up, and as a child it seemed to me that Big Momma's arms could reach way across town especially when I was about to get into trouble. She seemed to know my intentions even before I did something. She'd point her finger at me and tell me not to do something or not to mess with something. The next thing I knew, I'd be getting a whipping for doing what she told me not to do.

Whenever she heard about something terrible happening, Big Momma's response was that the world was coming to an end. When the *Titanic* sank, according to her it happened because the world was coming to an end. It really bothered me when she made comments like that. I'd look at her and say, "Big Momma, why just because you old the world's coming to an end and now I gotta die? I'm young and I want to live." She would just laugh and walk away, but the next time something happened, she'd say it again.

When Big Momma wasn't predicting the end of the world, she might be torturing any one of us girls with a comb. I had a lot of hair as a child and like most children, I hated getting my hair combed. It was dark red, thick, and very curly. Big Momma would sit me on the floor between her knees and she'd start to pulling. I'd holler, "Ahh!" and put my hand to my head to stop her. She'd whack me on the hand, scoot my back closer to her legs and tell me to move my hand. That woman was heavy handed whether she was using the comb or brush. It felt like she was trying to scrape off my scalp. It didn't really matter who was combing my tender head, it hurt so much. Sometimes it would bring me to tears just to get my hair combed. And I played so hard in the dirt and spent so much time outside looking for adventures and pets that I was doomed for a hair-combing session at least once a week.

Getting five squirming children from Habeshum Street to Franklin Square was no small task for my family even after a tasty breakfast of fried fish, hominy grits, and homemade rolls. Alonso was the eldest, then came Fredi, my big sister, then Robert, who we called Bubba, then me, and finally Rosebud, the baby. I'm Isabel, but everybody calls me Bel. My older siblings have gone on before me along with a number of precious friends. The longer I live, the more friends I lose. I think I've lost more than I can remember at this point. But life has been so good to me. God always sends me new friends and they do for me like they've known me all of my life.

Back in Savannah, each and every Sunday morning, our wagon headed for my least favorite place in town, the First African Baptist Church in Savannah. No matter what excuses I came up with, I found myself in God's house each and every Sunday, spic-and-span. I had Granddaddy, my father's father to blame. You see he was a deacon and had a number of responsibilities in the church. He beamed with pride at the mention of the church. He learned to read by studying the Bible. He taught us little verses from the good book, we blessed our food and prayed, and he made a great example for us, but we just never took to the church the way he had hoped.

Bringing his entire family to service was part of how Granddaddy showed his pride to the community and demonstrated that we weren't heathens. Even as a little girl, I knew there were some things you never wanted to be. One of them was a heathen. Thanks to my Granddaddy, we weren't. We went to church, read the Bible, and the pastor smiled at us on Sunday. All the deacons and their wives nodded their heads in approval when we passed their way.

Whenever we were around him, Granddaddy gave us his complete and undivided attention. He always had time for our million questions or to tell us a funny story with a happy ending. And even though I hated church, I loved that man. I can still smell the warm roasted peanuts he let slide into our little palms as he shook our hands. I never tire of peanuts even now and I will always think of him fondly as the Peanut Man.

Grandma Sara, my father's mother, was Granddaddy's wife. She and Little Momma, our mother, were all present in church too with the rest of the family, but it was Big Momma who made sure we minded during service. The dark wooden benches were hard, the service lasted longer than I could stay awake, and I never understood what the preacher was getting so excited about. It was either too hot - even with some of the church ladies directing a little air from their fans my way in the summertime - or too cold.

When I was awake, somehow I managed to squirm my way through the service without Big Momma giving me that look too many times. Occasionally the preacher would make an important announcement from the pulpit, something that would affect the entire community. There would be a mild rustling in the pews. Everyone would face front and lean forward. And someone would clear their throat as if they were the one about to speak. I would strain my ears to make sure I could hear. Usually I had no idea what was being said, but I didn't care. I might hear a new word and use it even though I didn't know what it meant. It was especially fun to say big words. They made me feel very grown up. Even back then, I was a nosy little something and wanted to know what was going on.

Heaven forbid if Big Momma had to tap me during any part of the service. And I'd better not cry out in the middle of church. Then I might not get to play in the lush green square in front when church let out. Acting up in church and embarrassing the family was a sign of a heathen. Even Granddaddy might have put us on punishment for that. In the holy house all the children were expected to be quiet and on their best behavior. Even the babies seemed to know that they were in a special place as their mothers hushed them.

I always wanted to stop and play in all the squares we passed on the way home. There were more squares than I could count, each just about the right size for a playing field, and covered with lush green grass. I would run from one end to the other, sometimes being chased by my brother, only to turn around and do it again. I screamed really loud if Bubba managed to touch the back of my dress. Then I would try to duck behind one of the tree trunks at the edge of the square. Their leaves were like little wings that I hoped to fly away on.

Except for church, and having to wear dress up clothes that we couldn't get too dirty, Sunday was a day I usually looked forward to. The parlor was open. The Georgia sun just about burned a hole in the curtains setting the entire room on fire, but I didn't care. It was that big black box in the back corner away from the window that was the object of my affection. It sat on a table, with the horn and handle facing the edge of the table. When they put on a record and turned that handle, I would lose myself in the dreamy music while my little body swayed from side to side. I could tell that the people singing those songs were happy, with smiles on their faces like in the stories that Granddaddy told us.

The only other place where we heard music regularly was at church. When people sang at church, their faces looked like they were in a lot of pain and whatever the problem was it couldn't be fixed. I preferred the music that came out of the black box, the Victrola. We weren't allowed to touch the box, so I spent hours staring at it and thinking about how nice it would be to climb up on a chair and play a record all by myself. Whenever I would almost work up the nerve to play a record, the picture of Jesus Christ on the wall seemed to stare at me from across the room. I was certain that He could see me and if I did anything, He would punish me for being a bad girl.

When company arrived, they would be led straight into the parlor as one of us kids fetched them a cool drink. This was the best part of the day because visitors usually brought gossip, and gossip was entertainment. My little heart would speed up just waiting to hear whatever news there was. One Sunday I was so busy minding grown folk's business that I leaned over too far on the banister and fell. When they heard the loud thump of my head hitting the bare wooden floor, they came a running. If it hadn't been for them thinking that I might have broken my neck or hurt myself really bad, I might still be on punishment to this day. Granddaddy of course hardly ever put us on punishment. He doted on us and created excuses so we could escape punishment if he were around. He was certain that whatever we had done wasn't intentional and that we were very sorry and just this once they should let it pass. Sometimes he would remind whoever we'd gotten in trouble with that he was a deacon at one of the oldest black churches in the country and that his judgment was sound. He was indeed the best granddaddy in the world. He also had the best job in the world.

All day long he got to ride up and down the elevator in the gents shoe store. How he had the patience to answer five faces full of questions after working all day, I do not know. We thought he knew everything. He mesmerized us with stories on the back porch where the cool breeze rustled the leaves on the trees creating a soft echo.

Bedtime always came too soon. Before we went inside, he'd point out the giant white ball floating in the sky, as if by magic, surrounded by blinking stars that lit up the universe. He pointed out the planets and told us their names. I climbed the stairs to my room wondering where the moon hid during the daytime and not understanding how the stars turned themselves on and off. Most of all I wondered how Granddaddy had gotten so smart and if I could be that smart when I grew up.

In addition to the heavens, Granddaddy had another hobby; he loved to read the newspaper. He clipped out every article he could find on the *Titanic* and others he thought were important. As a child, I remember people referring to the *Titanic* as the "unsinkable ship," and then discussing the tragedy of the sinking. It didn't make much sense to my young mind. Granddaddy had enough articles to write a book. He piled them up so high in the shed in the backyard that there was little room for anything else. I'm sure he never imagined that some of his own grandchildren would someday grace the very pages he read, and that their pictures would be right beside the story. He would have been so proud.

The only thing that would get Granddaddy out of the paper was Grandma Sara's vegetable soup. I tell you it was the tastiest soup in the world. They didn't have to tell us twice to eat our vegetables, not when it was Grandma Sara's soup. She was a quiet, warm and timid woman, but her soup made every taste bud in your mouth want to dance. We never tired of it. Each day after school the aroma of simmering soup greeted us at the door. To this day, when I eat soup, I think about Grandma Sara. My mouth waters and sometimes I have a second cup.

Grandma Sara got all her goodies for the soup from the market, a place of fascination for us kids. Brightly colored vegetables and fruit called to our eyes, while the aroma of herbs and spices made our noses flare. Many people spoke to us in English, but others spoke in Gullah (the West African and English-based language spoken in South Carolina and Georgia), which I understood fully as a child. When people spoke in Gullah it was as if they were singing, the words bouncing off their tongue. There were tabletops, crates low enough for me to peep into, and baskets covered with all manner of food. While Grandma eyed this, plucked that, and squeezed yet another vegetable, I looked around for treats.

Our family was a regular at the market. Vendors greeted us and called us over to see what they had as we entered the market. One Gullah woman in particular had taken a liking to our family. Grandma bought from her often. She usually carried two baskets, at least one on her head. She wore big cotton shirts with a low neck and great big pockets, and large puffy sleeves. Her colorful skirts fell all the way down to the ground. She was a pretty, dark-skinned girl with a sweet smile.

This lady would stop in front of me and call out something in Gullah. They were always talking about the wharf and what had just come in. She squatted down on the ground and took the baskets off her head. I looked at her green corn, okra, and tomatoes. The other basket held oysters, shrimps, and crabs. She'd call out to me again, almost singing and I would run back to Grandma and peek at the lady from behind her skirt. The lady would laugh and Grandma would select a few things from her. If we hadn't found a treat at the market, Grandma Sara gave us one when we got home.

Besides soup and peanuts, coffee is the single thing that reminds me of my grandparents. The strong aroma of the beans filled all three floors of our house daily. I remember sitting on Grandpa's lap while he sipped at the thin hot liquid like it was some kind of ambrosia. "I want some," I said in a small voice with a question mark at the end.

"Naw, you don't want any of this. Coffee will make you black like me," he said, taking another swig. I just looked at him trying to figure out what he'd just said and wondering why he wouldn't give me any of the drink he liked so much. I thought his rich smooth milk chocolate complexion was beautiful. It would take me years to understand the significance of his words and the sick way race and complexion are used against people. But he was my Granddaddy, a handsome picture of dignity. I wanted to be just like him. Now, hardly a day passes that I don't start my morning with coffee.

Like Granddaddy, my father worked in a shoe store. He

was the head stock clerk and prepared merchandise for delivery. He also worked a second job sorting mail at the Post Office. We called our father Daddy Pops. I don't know how he got the name. We've just always called him that. He was noticeably lighter skinned than Granddaddy, about 5'5" with a medium build. By today's standards he could have passed for white. What I remember most about him is that he was a kind and gentle man who took on domestic chores because our mother was sick.

There was nothing he wouldn't do for his kids. He washed dishes and straightened up the parlor. He did other tasks around the house when most men in this country refused to do "women's work." Nor did I ever hear him complain. He helped out by combing our hair, sometimes pulling it so tight we'd get little pimples around the temple. The backyard was his hair salon. That man could straighten hair without a hot comb. Maybe he didn't hear our cries because he was hard of hearing, or so he claimed. We believed he was only as deaf as he wanted to be, like when he combed our hair. And we never understood how being angry could improve his hearing.

Once he got so mad at Fredi he was going to whip her. She was about eight years old. I don't remember what Fredi had done or said to him, but when she looked at my father's tight face, she tore out of the house, hopped on her bike, and rode off down the street. Daddy took off after her on his own bike. Fredi headed for the park that we played in every Friday. She turned the corner heading for Big Momma's and safety. She couldn't pedal fast enough. Daddy was right on her tail as they wove in and out of traffic. Fredi was determined to escape and luck was on her side. At Big Momma's, she leaped off the bike and let it keep rolling, unguided, as she ran into the house and took refuge in our grandmother's apron. Daddy was only seconds behind and even more furious. Quickly sizing up the situation, Big Momma stood in the doorway separating him and Fredi. "Pick on somebody your own size," she told him. "I'm your size." Even though he was our daddy, he knew better than to challenge Big Momma, the undisputed boss of the family.

Fredi stood there looking past Big Momma at Daddy Pops, her little dress heaving up and down as she tried to catch her breath. Three pigtails hung from her head to her shoulders with matching ribbons at the ends, the picture of innocence.

The fire chief's family lived right next door to us. We were in and out of their house as much as they were in and out of ours. They were white. We were black. Like most children, we resembled our parents. All five of us were fair-skinned with what would be considered Caucasian features. My hair was thick, dark red and wavy, but Fredi's was almost straight and much finer. She had hazel eyes but Bubba's eyes were blue. All the girls were petite like our mother and even the boys weren't that big or tall. To us, these traits were little more than physical features we inherited from our parents. Both of them were black. Our looks did not make us any better or worse than our white neighbors or the blacks who lived across town. Clearly we were a light-skinned family, but we were also a black family – a proud black family. Everyone in town knew we were black and even more important; we knew it and celebrated the fact.

From the perspective of a five year old, we were just like everyone else, a normal family. I had no concept that people were judged and placed into categories based on race, complexion, hair texture, class and income. Most blacks lived on the other side of town, even Big Momma. But there was a lot of travel back and forth. Maybe we had been deemed "safe" because of how we looked or maybe nobody objected to us living here because we were a hard-working, church-going family, with good moral values. We didn't make any trouble. Whatever the reason, growing up in a white neighborhood and interacting with people on a regular basis, gave me confidence that I was just as good as anyone else. I deserved and should have the same opportunities as the next person. Maybe I was just too young and naïve to see things as they were. Fredi was older. She had a different experience.

I do know that we didn't create the sick system that rewards people who meet the accepted standard of white beauty and punishes those who don't. We would spend the rest of our lives fighting against the abuses of the system while at the same time enjoying the special privileges it allowed us. I know that's a bit of a contradiction, but I do not apologize. I am not to blame for my fabulous looks.

CHAPTER 2

Dr. Black Pill

When the summer was so hot and slow that kicking up dirt outside seemed exciting, we'd go to the Chinese laundry around the corner, pop our heads in, and tease the owner mercilessly before running away.

Chink, Chink, Chinaman
Eats dead rats
Won't save none
For the neighborhood cats,

we chanted. Our youthful ignorance allowed us to say such cruel things. If someone had made a similar comment about colored people, we would have wanted to fight. The wise Chinese man usually ignored us, knowing that we were bored children trying to provoke him. We would scurry back to Habeshum Street to see if anyone had a snack for us. The local baker, a German, had a shop on the corner. Granddaddy used to stop there frequently and bring home sweets. The baker's funny accent made us giggle but never stopped us from eating the delicious treats he made. When we tried to imitate how he spoke, we laughed for a long time because we could never get it quite right.

We were the only black family on the block in a predominantly white neighborhood. Other than us being colored and the others being white, for most of my early years I didn't perceive any difference between my family and the rest. Even in a Southern town like Savannah, I didn't understand what or who Jim Crow was other than it was something really bad. Adults talked about it in hushed tones which only made me perk up my ears more. But the pained looks on their faces while they swept their heads from side to side made me uneasy. What I did understand was that Jim Crow was not to be fooled with. Like many children, I was fortunate to be sheltered from the harshest realities of racism.

Race relations in the South were the least of our worries with Little Momma so sick most of the time. When she didn't have the energy to do basic chores around the house, to fix us something to eat, or read us a story, Grandma Sara would fill in. Daddy Pops would always help out when he got home from work. We tried to help as much as we could without getting in the way, but a lot of times we made even more of a mess.

From time to time we would give Grandma Sara a break and go next door to the Fire Chief's house. He had kids about our age. I played fashion consultant as my imagination coordinated outfits for my short thin paper models. My playmate's white long-haired dolls really captured my attention. They were so very pretty. And I had such fun dressing them up and combing their hair. Not once did it occur to me that I could not grow up to be one of them, beautiful, a permanent smile on my face, and everything right with the world. I claimed them as my own, shaking my head as her mother took them from my hands when it was time to go home.

We spent the weekends with Big Momma. She lived on Jones Street on the west side of town and always had more homemade goodies than we could eat. There were homemade breads, cakes, pies, and cookies. There was also ham, chicken and other slow-cooked meats. Everything she made was fabulous. My mouth would water just walking into the house. It smelled like a restaurant only it was Big Momma's place.

Fridays were an exception to our usual routine. Little Momma, who never chastised us, kept a chalkboard ledger of all of our offenses. The kitchen was on one side of the house attached to the rest by a narrow hallway. The blackboard sat in the hallway and any time I got ready to do anything I had no business doing, I would run up and see how many marks there were against my name. On Fridays Little Momma would carefully copy everything from the entire week and give the note to our baby sister, Rosebud, to carry. My name was always on the list. So to prolong getting it, we played in the park, as Rosebud sat on a bench holding our fate, a sense of mission on her little face.

In the park, my favorite brother, Bubba, pushed me on the swing as I squealed my delight. Sometimes he pushed me a little too hard and I'd go flying up in the sky, afraid that I'd fall, only to swing back the other way so his hands could meet my back again.

But I always had confidence that he'd never let anything bad happen to me, not unless he did it himself. Like the time my little life was almost snuffed out with a pillow because I was screaming and carrying on to everyone's annoyance, and for no apparent reason. He just wanted to shut me up, not kill me. But that day in the park, my screams of delight mixed with laughter for what seemed like hours until it was time to go to Big Momma's. I dragged my feet into the house hoping to somehow avoid my fate.

Before dinner, Big Momma held court. She read every word of Little Momma's note, attaching the offense to each child's bottom with her eyes. Dinner would be great, the best food this side of heaven. I tried to eat real slow. Then Big Momma would lecture us about making Little Momma's life so difficult, causing us to burst into tears. While we were still sniffling, one of us would be told to retrieve Dr. Black Pill, a horrible instrument of torture with a handle and five leather straps. One by one if our names were listed, we went into the bedroom. It was hard to go get Dr. Black Pill. My lips would be poked out and the rest of my face would fall into a frown. But I didn't dare say I couldn't find it or make some other excuse. Then my fate would be even worse. Discipline, respect, and doing what you were told were ways of life.

I was always last. The second Big Momma looked my way; I'd start to hollering and take off running. I screamed long and hard before she even touched me, like it was Judgment Day. I went over the bed, and around the furniture, and back under the bed until Dr. Black Pill caught up with me. Lord, she had a time with me. When I felt the lash of Dr. Black Pill, my screams were loud enough to convince anyone within earshot that my own grandmother was trying to kill me. If anyone from outside ever did hear me, they never came to my rescue, not even once. My grandmother would not have been the least bit surprised that I got involved in the theater. I gave her quite a few dramatic performances.

While our butts still burned, grandma sat us down for lemonade and cake. If we resisted through our sniffles, she'd give us a look with hunched eyebrows and threaten to give us something to cry about. So we ate, slow and full of resentment, but we ate.

The next morning she'd try to make up, but I wanted no part of it. She'd greet us with a big smile and a warm breakfast hug. "Well, good morning Ma Bel!" she'd say to me. Then she'd go into the backyard and pick one of those sugar-sweet Georgia peaches off the tree. My mouth would start to water as soon as I could see it, but I would turn my eyes away knowing how bad I wanted it. I loved those peaches more than anything in the world, but I couldn't give in to her, not while my behind still hurt. I'd purse my lips shut, refusing her offer of peace.

"I don't want it," I'd say, with my lips pouting. She'd press the ripe fruit to my lips until the juice ran down my chin. She warned me that I'd better eat the peach. Right Now! Soon enough I'd be devouring the sweet peach and getting it all over my dress. Grandma was happy. And I had temporarily forgotten that she had whipped my butt real good. But not for a moment did I fool myself into believing that the scenario would not repeat itself each and every weekend of my childhood. So each Friday I would stay in the park as long as possible.

If she felt that I was really hurt, Big Momma would let us go out and play. I loved being outside where I might find a new pet and where we played all kinds of games as grandma worked her artistry in the kitchen. My brother, Bubba knew I hated crawly things. Little animals I loved, but anything that crawled was not for me. Bubba made a habit of digging up worms and chasing me with them. I was terrified but loved the attention. When you're a little kid with a big brother you adore, he can do anything he wants to you, just as long as he doesn't ignore you. When Bubba couldn't find worms or was too lazy to bother, he'd hang around the kitchen, take the pieces of leftover dough, roll them into shape, and rub them in dirt. They looked exactly like worms. The better to chase me with. He chased, and I ran screaming, with a smile on my face as wide as one of the boulevards.

I loved playing with my siblings, but nothing thrilled me more than finding a new four- legged friend outside. Several of the neighbors knew I loved animals and gave me pets from time to time. Someone actually gave me a baby alligator once. I took it home and put it under the bed where I thought it would be safe. I was so excited to have a pet with a puzzle on its back. It was only a few inches long, had a cute little mouth fixed in a smile, and the scales on its back formed a colorful pattern. It never occurred to me that my alligator might grow big enough to eat someone some day. It looked more like a lizard to me. I caught little flies and insects and gave it to the baby. I had a pan of water there for it and I talked to it like it was a real baby. It would turn its little head to listen to me. It needed attention.

I made sure to check on my little pet before leaving the house. It seemed content resting under my bed. When Big Momma went in there to clean, she drew the bed covers back. She saw the pan underneath the bed and then something wiggled. She looked under the bed to see what had moved and nearly lost her mind. It still makes me laugh when I think about her letting out a loud scream, but I just couldn't get over what she did. She got rid of my pet. When I found out I tried hard not to forgive her. I refused to smile if she was in the room. And I wouldn't give her a hug. I literally cried for weeks. I took these things very personally even as a young child. But eventually I forgave her as I searched for my next pet.

One day a neighbor sent for me to come over right away. Her big mouse had had babies. I was thrilled. When she gave me one I screamed and hugged her tight. I couldn't thank her enough. My baby mouse was pink. It was the tiniest most precious little thing. It didn't have any hair yet. I felt sorry for it. But it wouldn't have to worry because I would take good care of it. The neighbor put it in a small candy dish. Back then, candy came in little dishes with a spoon. It cost a penny or so. We would eat the candy and use the dish for something else. I took it home in a little woven waste paper basket. I was so happy Big Momma was going to let me keep it. I could barely stop myself from checking on it every few minutes to make sure it was okay. I had to be its mommy because it didn't have one.

At one point, Fredi and Bubba were quarantined. They had something like chicken pox. We had to hand Fredi her food at the door to the bedroom. She used to sit at the window because she couldn't come outside and play. I was so proud of my new pet. I stood outside and showed her my mouse. She cried and screamed and hollered. "Don't bring me any food. Don't let her near me. I don't want that thing in the house." She didn't want anything to do with me or my mouse. Oh, was she ever upset.

Before I went to bed, I put some water in the candy dish, and put my pet in his basket. Then I laid my clothes on the back of the chair in our room and put my shoes underneath. Big Momma didn't like it if we let our rooms get too messy. I had to be on my best behavior, with my new little friend in the house. I climbed into bed after saying my prayers, knowing I would get up in the morning and play with my mouse.

I woke up and went right over to check on the baby. When my little body let out a giant scream, Big Momma came running into the room. My tiny adorable mouse had turned over the dish of water and drowned itself. I was heartbroken. Fredi always said I was too preoccupied with the humble little creatures. She just didn't appreciate my sensibilities when it came to little ones.

CHAPTER 3

Fredi

Big sisters are kind of like men, experts at everything and wrong about nothing. They protect you from harm only so they can annoy you to death themselves. Fredi was no different. She always had something to say about my actions, but I'll let her tell you in her own words.

As a child, my darling little sister Isabel was consistently unmanageable. Today, she is one of the best-groomed women I know. But back in our hometown, Savannah, she was the dirtiest kid in the neighborhood. She still gets upset when I say it – but it's the gospel truth. Some of the neighbor kids used to tease her. They'd put their hats on when she joined their play. Claimed she had lice in her hair.

No doubt you've heard of children who bring stray animals home. Isabel was absolutely ridiculous! She was always discovering various small forms of animal life and inflicting them upon her family. Once, her pride in small pets and love of teasing almost got her killed and me the tragic honor of having murdered my sister. Naturally, I never intended to do Isabel any harm. I loved her dearly, but I am not a passive person. I flew into a blind rage the morning she played a dirty trick on me. She marched noisily into my bedroom, waking me up. She wore a dear little sister look on her face which, from bitter experience, should have made me suspicious. She was carrying a tray almost as big as she was and I thought: "Oh, the little sweetheart. She's serving me breakfast in bed."

The smile of contentment got wiped off my face fast and was replaced by what must have been a prize portrait of horror.

Nestling cozily among the dishes on my breakfast tray was a tiny white mouse. My heartbeat quickened with fear and fury. Isabel knew how I loathed mice, even tiny mice. They sent me up the wall. They still do.

"Surprise!" Isabel shrieked merrily. She had the gall to be standing there laughing, her mischievous eyes dancing. I became temporarily insane. Our brother, Bubba, was standing in the doorway. He'd been invited along to witness this monstrous surprise. I was trembling with revulsion and rage. I dashed over to the fireplace, snatched up a red hot poker from the burning coals and sailed it straight at Isabel's head. Thank God she ducked just in time. If it had struck home, my baby sister would never have grown up to be a beautiful and sexy Broadway musical comedy star, to become the subject of newspaper headlines when she met and married Adam Clayton Powell Jr.

The incident with the white mouse was only one of Isabel's adventures with these humble creatures. One of her pet mice died and you would have thought we'd had a death in the family. That child carried on so. When she had exhausted her physical grief, she began planning the little vermin's last rites. The mouse was laid to rest in a cigar box lined with cellophane and paper rings you get off of cigars or cigarette packs. The funeral was held in the backyard and Isabel had intimidated half the neighborhood into coming to pay their respects. She dug a hole in the yard and carefully placed the "coffin" in the grave. All the kids were crying. She was something. She constantly had something going on and the minute she'd get into trouble, she'd come running straight to me. My little sister.

Isabel did get into more trouble than the rest of us, but I had my moments too, like the time I didn't make the ball team. It was my attempt to liberate the sexist sport of baseball. I wanted to play with my brothers and their friends. But they made it clear that I was neither wanted nor needed. I thought I had won them over with my persistence when they stationed me behind the batter. I guess they had already worked out what they were going to do.

Here I was a girl, playing baseball with the boys! One of them came up to bat. I tried to watch every move so I'd be ready for anything. He swung hard, hit the ball, and kept right on around with the bat until he literally knocked me out. The dull thud of wood slamming against flesh created a thousand festival lights and stars in my head. They picked me up, tossed me over to the side out of the way, and went on with their game. So much for integrating baseball.

As the oldest girl I was sent on errands for the family on a regular basis. Sometimes Isabel wanted to come but I was

16

glad to have a break from my noisy, disaster-prone younger sister. Everywhere she went, trouble followed. It was her shadow. Back then, money had a lot more weight. With a pound of coffee no longer having a price but a ransom, I think back fondly on those "good old days" when a nickel was worth five cents. It really was incredible what you could do with just a nickel. The top bargain on my list was buttermilk. I loved the stuff. I'm not talking about this cultured, counterfeit substance they call buttermilk these days. When we said buttermilk, we were talking about a creamy, white liquid in which you could see the pure butter floating on top. Little Momma had often sent me to the nearby dairy with a two-quart milk can which would be filled to the top for a nickel. More times than one, I'd sample this delicious stuff so greedily on the way home that I'd have to find someone to loan me a nickel so I could get the can refilled and take it home.

Another thing about a nickel. You could get on the bus and ride all over town for five cents. While I didn't know about the social implications of racism, I did know about the Rules. Black kids got to learn early about those Rules because, even if you were light of skin as most of my family was, to the white people you were something beneath them. Some of them were nice and cool and smooth about it, others were just plain nasty. Whatever their manner, the racism usually seemed to be present. The only way you could survive it was by knowing the Rules.

There were a lot of Rules, but one of the most important stipulated that blacks did not ride on the public streetcar, except when absolutely necessary. You could get on and ride all over town for a nickel. If you did, you were expected to sit or stand only in the back. When the car was filling up, white folks could take our seating space, but we didn't dare take theirs – even if everyone on the streetcar was black. You drank "black" water because the signs in the fountains were clearly marked "For Whites" and "For Niggers." Some places, the signs were a little more cool. They read "For Colored" rather than "For Niggers."

I'm sure I had no deep awareness of the twisted way the system operated against black people. Certainly, I did not fancy myself as a crusader, but recalling those days in Savannah, I feel a certain pride in my youthful daring. At the age of eleven, I made a bold attempt at integrating a bus. It was about as successful as my attempt to integrate baseball. Apparently, nobody gave a damn that I was a midget militant and a heroine.

The city was bringing in small, fast, efficient conveyances – jitney buses, we called them. They would ultimately replace the tired old streetcars. Among the black folks, it was a foregone conclusion

17

that the jitneys were for white folks. *They were excitingly new looking. They were fast and they looked neat. I heard grown-ups say that they knew "Mr. Charlie" did not intend for us colored folks to ride those new jitneys. They were so small and had a lot less seats than streetcars. It was logical that, if we were only tolerated in the back of the regular streetcars and buses, there'd be no room for us in those jitneys.*

I couldn't accept the idea. I was smart enough not to say the way I felt about it around the family. But I had made up my mind I was going to ride one of those smart new jitney buses whether they wanted me to or not. I took a nickel out of my coin saver, went to the corner and waited. The bus arrived. I stepped on. I took a seat up front and settled down awaiting adventure. Absolutely nothing happened. People acted as though I wasn't even there. The ride was neat, but it wasn't turning out to be the thrill I expected. I got off and walked slowly back home.

In the South, race was always an issue no matter how light you were. People were very wary about racial mixing and everyone, even kids, seemed to want to look down on someone else. Hence I have to admit that we sometimes teased the Chinese man who owned the laundry sometimes. I did not recognize it as a racist practice back then but I do now. We didn't have to tiptoe around our neighborhood or anything. Everyone knew we were black and we were NOT passing, but I did have one direct but brief confrontation with racial hostility.

I was having fun on my skateboard one day. It was not one of these elaborate contraptions of today. It had a long handle on it and was rather like a scooter. I was happily minding my own affairs when along came this little cracker kid. He sang out something to the effect that I was a "dirty little nigger." Promptly I swung off my skateboard, lit into him and tried my best to murder him. I punched him harder when I saw that it was Clabberfoot, that's what we called the German baker's son. Then I retrieved my skateboard and resumed my interrupted play. I'd not heard the names Gandhi or Dr. King and I've never been non-violent. My family patronized the bakery shop regularly. But for me, if we weren't clean enough to pass beside on the road, then neither was our money. I never quite looked at the shop the same after that. And when Daddy Pops or someone brought sweets home, I'd often pass and offer them to Isabel and Rosebud.

For most of the few years we children lived in the South, we knew very little of racial ugliness. We were too young. We were sheltered and protected from it. We did not move in circles or engage in activities where bigotry would confront us. I tried hard to help protect the ones under me, especially Isabel and Rosebud. Even when I was hurting, I hid it from them. They shouldn't see that. It seemed no matter what happened, I was getting slapped in the face either because of my race or my gender. All I could do was hang in there and fight. Things were bound to change, they had to.

⟜⟋

From as far back as I can remember, I looked up to Fredi and wanted to be like my big sister. I'm not talking about the sharp angles of her cheekbones, her blue-hazel eyes, or delicate hands. I'm talking about the way she always made life seem easy and fun. She seemed so grown up and proper. She had all the answers. Nothing could shake her. She was in control. Big words rolled off her tongue with no effort. And if she wanted you to do something, she would not let up until it was done. As pretty as she was, she also had a tough tomboy side to her. She would fight absolutely anybody who messed with us. And, yes, she usually won. The only people she seemed to fear were Daddy Pops and Big Momma. Sometimes she was able to avoid punishment by playing one against the other.

She was always prepared, no matter what was happening. She was so sure of herself. I can hardly remember a single time when she didn't know what to do. Even her birthday was exciting to me. She was born on December 23rd, 1903, two days before Christmas. I thought how much fun it must be to have a birthday and then to have a major holiday a couple of days later, another celebration. The fact is, instead of twice the fun and twice the gifts; she didn't always get two separate gifts. I usually did, but my birthday is May 23rd, nowhere near any major holiday.

Even her name made her stand out. She was the pretty girl who had a boy's name. No one really called her Fredericka, except Big Momma or Daddy Pops when she had done something bad and they used that serious tone. It was always just Fredi, plain and simple, but special for her.

We were only a few years apart, but she was wise beyond her years as the old folks used to say. When I felt down, she knew just what to say. She even managed to make me smile sometimes not long after Big Momma gave me a good whipping. The smile would lead to a giggle about something else, and soon enough I would have forgotten about my whipping and be headed for my next mess.

Even though I wasn't but knee high to an adult, I could see that people were drawn to Fredi. She seemed to have some kind of magic power. When she looked at people, they were captured by her stare. She put people in a trance, calmed them down, and made everything alright. Her friends came to her for advice and came back to thank her after it worked. No matter what she was doing, she was always beautiful. If she had curlers in her hair, the light caught her eyes so that she looked stunning, just like our Little Momma. Outside on her scooter, she was the picture of balance and grace. I would fall down when I tried it and she'd come scoop me up and make the scratch go away.

Maybe it's the memories I have of my mother that make me adore my sister so very much. Whenever I was around Fredi, I knew I was safe and that everything would be taken care of. I wanted to have some of the same power Fredi had, to make people feel good, have them attracted to me, to make them feel better, but that was her gift not mine. What I did have was a terrific comic flair and a sense of drama. I used those talents to try to get the same results Fredi got. Even though I consider her the master and me the understudy, I've had a few successes as I remain in training. Sometimes she was more like a mother hen than a sister, but she was always a good friend. God could not have given me a better big sister.

CHAPTER 4

Cakewalk

My father, Daddy Pops, was unlucky with women. Not that he couldn't find a good one; he actually found three. Hattie Washington, my mother, was his first love. We called her Little Momma. I was only a little tyke about five when she passed away but I can still see her face. My older sister Fredi looked just like her; petite, fair-skinned, with soft wavy hair, light eyes, and slender fingers. She was a beautiful woman. Poor little Rosebud was only about three years old when Little Momma left us. She can barely remember her at all.

At home Little Momma was always tired. The slightest exertion and she would have to sit down and take a moment to catch her breath. The normal things a mother does for her children, Little Momma couldn't do for us. She didn't have the energy. She had to be real careful about even picking us up. Her health was delicate as they say. Each summer she went off to "the country," but her health never seemed to improve. Maybe us kids were too much for her.

When Little Momma went away on her trips, Daddy Pops moved around the house in a daze. He went through all the motions but his eyes were sad and he wasn't focused on whatever he was doing. He tried to hide it from us, the idea that one day she might not come back. So he smiled when he rode his bicycle, tickled us, and helped out around the house while we did our school work. If we were about to do something we had no business doing he might say, "Little Momma wouldn't want you to do that," and instantly we would change our minds. We would have done almost anything not to disappoint her.

Somehow Big Momma and Daddy Pops managed to keep the house running smoothly in Little Momma's absence. Of course,

Grandma Sara and Granddaddy helped out too. Even though Little Momma couldn't do a lot of house work and chastising us was out of the question, her sheer presence was the lifeblood of our household. When she returned, armfuls of gifts always brought smiles to our faces. Each time she came home, five small faces crowded around her in the vain hope that this visit had cured her of whatever ailment she had. She wanted to know what we had done, where we had been, and if we had minded while she was away. We all wanted to speak at once, so she would take one of our hands and that child would speak first. Despite the frequent separations that chipped away at the instinctive bond we had with our mother, we loved and missed her terribly when she left for "the country" and were overjoyed when she returned.

Like a magic pill, when the circus or carnival came to town, Little Momma's illness almost seemed to disappear. For a few days she was in a sunny mood and somehow found the energy to even compete. Her movement was effortless, like she was doing an activity that she was born for. She brought her knees up high to her chest and kept a small grin on her lips. The picture of balance and grace, Little Momma did the cakewalks and always won. The prize was a lovely cake. Before she married my father and had all of us kids, she had won enough cakes to open her own bakery. Fredi and I must have inherited her talent because we had no formal dance training of any kind. Unfortunately, the happy diversions were only a temporary break from her illness. Soon after the smiling faces of the clowns faded, Little Momma would fall sick again.

She never let her illness undermine her love and concern for her children. One time my older brother, Bubba, got out of the house. He could not have been any more than three or four years old. Little Momma was in a panic looking for him. She ran out of the house and headed down Overthaw Boulevard. It was a wide avenue, populated by well-to-do families who lived in houses right beside each other. Everyone knew that we were a colored family even though our complexions were light. Little Momma must have been something running down the street screaming for someone named Bubba.

There was no sign of my brother. My mother was frantic. Finally she passed a house and overheard two women arguing.

"I saw him first," said the first voice.

"No, I saw him first," said the other voice even more emphatic. "He belongs to me."

My mother knocked on the blinds and a woman opened the door. My brother, who climbed down from the chair where he was sitting when he saw Little Momma, wore the cutest short suit and bow tie any boy has ever worn. My mother walked right in and explained that he actually belonged to her. They gave him back reluctantly. Little Momma brought him home wondering what two well-to-do white women wanted with a little colored boy. Even though he had blue eyes and light hair, there was no mistaking that he was colored. All of us children knew the story. It could have been any one of us that Little Momma risked her life for. She would not rest until she found him. It was just the kind of activity that would have completely tired her out. She loved us all the same, but we teased Bubba about it every chance we got.

Not long after Bubba's return, we heard the "Whoa!" from Aunt Mabel, Big Momma's sister. This single word was the warning signal to run and hide. Even though I loved animals, I took off running as soon as I heard her distinctive voice followed by the sound of horse hooves. She drove a noisy wagon like the ones you see on television in the old cowboy movies. At least twice a year she came by the house to dole out medication that was supposed to "clean us out." Castor oil with hot water was the only treat she offered. Even though I tried my best to block the spoon with tightly pursed lips, she'd just scrape the stuff off my face and neck, and tell me I was going to swallow every drop. She always had a time with me. I would never impose that stuff on anybody, let alone on a child. Even now, the mere thought of castor oil makes my stomach turn.

As if her winter visits weren't enough, she'd come back in the spring and force us to swallow sulphur and molasses. Of course, my reaction was the same. I didn't want anything she said was good for me, even if it did keep me healthy. If castor oil and sulphur were so good, Little Momma would have taken some and it would have made her all better. God knows she was sick enough for the entire family. The only thing I hated worse than Aunt Mabel's visits was a few moments with Dr. Black Pill, that little bit of time would surely cure your body of whatever ailed you.

Daddy Pops came home one day and we could immediately tell that something was really wrong. His face was very tight and we could feel that he was all torn up inside. He gave us a tight hug and went into the parlor. The neighbors said it was a terrible thing that my mother met her fate so young. From the perspective of a five year old, someone in their thirties was ancient. Grown-ups used big words and had a way of talking to disguise what they were saying. I found it very frustrating because I always liked to know what was going on. At five years old, I wasn't exactly sure what "meeting one's fate" was.

Rosebud and I stopped our play when they brought a

wooden pine box into the parlor. I knew they put people in those boxes when they died, because my great grandfather had me lie in one to measure a box for a child about my size. But like most children, I didn't really understand the concept of death. Back then, people were not embalmed. Instead, family members or neighbors bathed and dressed the body which was laid out in the parlor or front bedroom for viewing.

Rosebud and I peeked through the banister rail and tried to figure out why so many people were coming and going to the house - droves of people with long faces and puffy eyes. Rosebud sat near the bottom step and I was a bit higher up. We had been told that Little Momma had gone away and would not be coming home ever again, but we just couldn't figure out what that meant. Finally we went to Fredi, who, we called Sister. She knew everything. Children can take such things very personal. We wanted to make sure we hadn't done anything ourselves to make our mother go away. In the past when she had gone away she had always come back. Fredi fought back tears and told us how much Little Momma loved us but she would not be coming back. Even her words of comfort came up short.

The house swarmed with neighbors and friends come to pay their respects. Along with the people came pots and pans overflowing with food, cakes and pies in more varieties than we could identify, and large containers of cool and hot sweet drinks. There was so much stuff; it almost seemed like a party. And yet we knew that this was not an occasion to celebrate. People hugged our little bodies and reassured us all day. Everything would be okay they said.

When they told us Little Momma had died, the only thing I understood was that she wouldn't be coming back to us. She had always come back before. A truck was usually packed up with her things and we had gotten used to her leaving often. I didn't understand why this time should be any different. Apparently Little Momma had had some kind of operation and something went wrong. Medical science back then was not quite what it is today.

For a long time after her death, I lay awake at night and prayed for three things; that Little Momma had gone somewhere where she wouldn't be so sick; that Daddy Pops would lose that sad look hiding behind his eyes; and that Fredi would hurry up and tuck me in, like Little Momma used to do. From that night on, Sister became a parent to the rest of us. Just a few years older, she was little more than a child herself, but her childhood ended as she took on the responsibility of looking after us. Much later Sister explained that Little Momma had gone to heaven. She was in heaven. Somehow when I heard those words from Sister they began to sink in. Heaven was that place they talked about in church just before they turned their eyes upward and shook their heads from side to side with the pained looks on their faces. If Little Momma was in heaven then she must be okay.

My mother's death when I was such a tender age taught me that I could survive any hurt, no matter how deep. I'm sure I must have resented losing her so young, but my large family tightened its circle and filled in the empty spaces created by my mother's absence. While no one ever took my mother's place, between Big Momma and Fredi, I never felt deprived of maternal love. Sometimes I can still see her. Her long dark hair is pinned up high on her head away from her soft delicate face. The high-necked collar of her embroidered blouse is covered in lace. Her skirt, fitted tight at her tiny waist, falls gracefully to her ankles and has buttons all the way down the front. The petticoats underneath add a bit more fullness to the skirt. This is how my Little Momma lives on in my memory.

For a long time after Little Momma's death it seemed like all the fun had been taken out of life. The adults stumbled around the house trying to make sense of things. Nothing was ever the same. Grandma Sara's vegetable soup didn't taste good. I didn't want to go to school and even when I did it was hard to sit still for more than a few minutes. I only wanted to stay around my family. That was the only safe and secure place where I didn't have to worry about losing anyone else. Nothing seemed to matter to me. Not even my pets gave me any solace.

I still got into mischief just like before but not nearly as much. Big Momma took pity on me and didn't whip me as often. We didn't hear her say, "Walk beyond your Hinishey, come here," at all for a while. That was the warning that you were going to get a licking. So when we heard it, we tried to go the other way. She would reach for us and we'd start backing away. I never found out where she got the funny phrase but I was awful glad not to hear it for a time. For a good little while, things were pretty quiet over at the Washington house over on Habeshum Street.

As one day turned into the next, we began to fall back into our family routine. Daddy Pops taught Fredi how to go to market. Like him she loved to ride her bicycle so he taught her how to market on her bicycle. I was only a few years younger, and I wish he had taught me too. She looked so grown up in her wide hat, carrying a big basket. He gave her what seemed like a lot of money to me. It was just a few dollars for shopping, but that went a long way back then. Fredi looked just like Little Momma. When I grew up I wanted to be just like Fredi.

People had already had a time with me, but after Little Momma died, I became even more rambunctious. I made a constant fuss about going to church. I didn't care about heaven or hell; I just wanted Little Momma back. She was my mother and she was supposed to take care of me, of us. Big Momma and Fredi were always ready with a hug and a kind word, but sometimes even they didn't know what to do with me. Fredi did everything she could but she had her own life too. Big Momma was getting up in age and could only do so much with the several kids.

Slowly, very slowly, at some point we decided that it was okay to miss Little Momma but to keep on living. A little bit of joy seeped back into our lives and we began to smile again. We let go of our self-pity and the family made plans for our future. Fredi and I might be going away to a nice school, how exciting!

Occasionally, Daddy Pops would have to go out for something and no adults were in the house. Fredi didn't waste any time taking charge. She had promised Little Momma on her death bed that she would take care of us and Fredi did not intend to go back on her word.

One time Daddy Pops left us alone. The neighbor where we used to go and play came over to look in on us. She was probably more concerned than anything. She told Fredi, "Now, look after Isabel, don't let anything happen to her." I don't know what got into Fredi, but she gave the woman a hard look and demanded, "You mind your business and I'll mind my business!" She slammed the door in the woman's face. Fredi was older than us but she was still a little girl. We had been taught to mind our elders and what have you, but that day, Fredi was "the elder". After that day, I knew I didn't have to worry about a thing when Fredi was in charge.

As we began to adjust to life without Little Momma, we worked hard to get back to normal. The adults started going out again. A few people stopped by the house to visit, and there was always church. Daddy Pops, Big Momma, and Fredi took care of us and made us believe that we would somehow survive. Little by little my father started to laugh again. I noticed because it took so long for it to happen.

It was so good to see Daddy Pops in a good mood. I was too young to recognize it at the time, but the kind of smile in his eyes and pep in his step usually comes from seeing a woman. He may have begun to date my future stepmother but all I knew is that he was happy. It made me laugh. Big Momma remained the strong rock of the family, Grandma Sara made great soup again, and Granddaddy told fascinating stories and piled up more newspapers. Things were as back to normal as they could be without Little Momma here.

Years later, after I had left Savannah, Granddaddy began to lose his mind. Maybe he had some form of what we call Alzheimer's today. One day he took his newspaper clippings that he valued so much and began to hammer and nail them to the front of the house. Finally he let someone lead him inside. It wasn't long after that that he died. When I heard about his passing I thought about my Little Momma who had gone on years before. I decided that I would remember him as he was just before he retired. At night when he got ready to go to bed, he would have a small piece of cheese and an apple. Then he would give each of us a loving night-night embrace before marching off to bed. He was a tall, proud, dignified man and that's how I cherish his memory.

CHAPTER 5

The Piglet's Pardon

Only Catholics have more names than they can use in a single lifetime. Mine is Isabel Marion Mary Rosemarie Theodore Washington, but my friends call me Bel. The nuns at Holy Providence insisted on calling me Isabel, another formality on the long list of things I hated about the place. Children who'd lost their mother were considered orphans because men were ill-equipped to raise children, or so they claimed. Whether my father could not handle the constant reminder of my mother in Fredi's face, or he was merely concerned that we grow up to be proper young ladies, I do not know. Shortly after our mother's death, however, Fredi went to a Catholic convent in Cornwell Heights, Pennsylvania.

St. Elizabeth's Convent, also known as Holy Providence, was run by the Reverend Mother Katharine Biddle. The convent took in Native American and colored orphans. I certainly didn't consider myself an orphan. I had Daddy Pops and Big Momma, but she was up in age and couldn't possibly be expected to raise all of us. So Fredi was sent to the orphanage. I followed in due time. Rosebud, the baby, and my brothers stayed at home with Big Momma.

I had never been away from home before for any extended period of time. My family thought it best that I go away for a while to prepare for the convent, so to speak. I went to Washington, D.C. where we had an aunt and uncle. They lived near Howard University. I was excited about going to a new place even though my siblings wouldn't be there. I decided that I had better try to make the most of it. Maybe I could even keep out of trouble. They enrolled me in Lucretia Mott Elementary School. It was down the street from

Freedman's Hospital on Fourth Street. The school was named for an abolitionist who also fought for women's rights. I was in the fourth grade.

I was not a shy kid but making friends was harder than I thought. The kids made fun of me. They called me "four eyes" because now I had these awkward glasses that made my eyes look big. They mimicked my Southern accent before falling over laughing. I would show them. More than once I had to tell kids to meet me out back of the school after class where I would try my best to beat them silly. It didn't matter if it was a boy or girl. They would think twice about teasing me again. Little Momma was gone and Fredi wasn't here for me to run to. I had to defend myself. I had learned to fight from watching Fredi. If she could do it, I could do it too.

I was no more interested in my lessons than I had been before. The name calling and the fights only made it worse. This new place was not going so well but there was a bright moment. One of the girls in my class named Elyse was nice to me. She tried to get the kids to stop teasing me. She thought that was mean. I think she was from D.C. We became friends. She was small like me with light skin and wavy hair. But she seemed to enjoy school and actually liked her lessons. She was smart. By the time I was getting settled in and used to the place, it was time to leave for the convent. I would miss my new friend but I couldn't wait to go. Sister was there! I knew it would be great.

Given our Baptist upbringing, Catholicism was a strange new adventure for me. Fredi didn't seem to mind the place at all. I marveled at my big sister as she bowed, recited verses, and did everything perfectly as though she had been doing it all of her life. She had already adjusted to the strict routine by the time I got there. Her conversion was smooth and without resistance. My conversion, on the other hand, was lumpy and remains incomplete. Most of all, I hated the discipline of the place.

Neither the Father, the Son, nor the Holy Ghost concerned me at the crack of dawn when nuns came into our room and splashed cold water on our faces. I knew I would have to find a way out of the place after the first time they did that. Nor was I willing to kneel at the nuns' feet on the cold barren floor when they called those sacred names. I wanted to tell my family how much I hated the place, but they censored our mail. I was trying hard to be good because I knew the predicament our family was in. Still, I cried frequently and gave the Sisters such a time that they bent the rules a little and let me room with Fredi. They had actually moved a girl out of Fredi's room so I could be near her.

I have never flourished in environments where someone else dictated what I could and could not do and when. Whether it was chores, prayers, or wearing that awful uniform, I gave them a time at every turn. God gave us free will, so why couldn't they give us a little bit of choice somewhere? Maybe Holy Providence had never encountered such a free spirit. I was too troubled to master my lessons but I knew that I didn't belong there. I couldn't believe that I had actually been excited about the place at first. Going away to school had sounded like fun. It turned out to be more like a military camp. I wanted no part of it.

One day I was walking around and found a little kitten. Given my penchant for taking care of little animals, of course I took it in. There was a baby carriage sitting around which I placed the kitten in after I found some baby clothes for it. I thought I was doing a kind, considerate, sweet thing. When a young nun saw me with the kitten in the carriage, she kicked the carriage! I had to bite down hard on my teeth to keep from yelling at her. I was so mad. The poor baby kitten ran up a tree and I just wanted to cry. I knew I had to behave, or else. I had to find a way out of this crazy place.

Just after I had gotten over the kitty kicking nun incident, it was time for me to be baptized. They told me ahead of time not to look directly at the priest. I never understood why the priest could look at me but I couldn't look at him. He was a man, flesh and blood just like me. As far as I was concerned, this was just one more piece of evidence that I did not belong in this place. I became even more resentful after my baptism.

Not even visits from home could induce me to conform. On one visit, my father brought up Rosebud and a woman he introduced as my new stepmother. Her name was Daisy and right away I didn't like her. While I was happy he had found someone who made him laugh and smile again, I couldn't help but feel a twinge of resentment toward this stranger who now commanded my father's affections. I kept telling myself that she was no relation to me. Besides, Little Momma was much prettier. I wasn't trying to be mean, but I resisted her attempts to be friendly and get to know me.

Daddy Pops was a full grown adult as well as my father, but part of me was angry at him for not asking my permission to marry this new woman. The least he could have done was discuss it with us before he actually married her. Didn't we still matter? We had already lost Little Momma. I refused to lose him to some stranger. It wasn't fair.

Fredi was her usual charming self. Daddy Pops' new wife didn't seem to bother her much. I felt better after they said goodbye and headed for the train. Daddy Pops had closed my fingers around a few mints, which he always carried, and told me I would eventually adjust to Holy Providence. I just had to give the place an honest chance. I loved my father with all my heart. I really wanted this to work out for all of us. But couldn't he see how miserable I was here - how desperate I was to get away?

Visits home were another story. I always looked forward to them. They were the only real breaks I had from that place. Visiting friends and neighbors was always a breath of fresh air. A few times I went to visit people but the family had moved away, had gone north to fancy places like Pennsylvania and New York, places that I could only dream about. I'd head home to play with Rosebud, making sure I picked up a few penny candies from the corner store. When Fredi and I visited, we tried to do something special with her. We wanted to make sure Rosebud got the attention she needed, and we didn't know how preoccupied my father was with his new wife. Her sad eyes always lit up at the sight of our faces. I was only a tiny thing myself when Little Momma left us, but Rosebud, poor thing, she might not be able to remember her at all. Fredi and I had to fill in the gaps. Whatever she needed, we would be there. Fredi, of course, was like a mother hen looking after both of us.

On one of our trips home, the family announced that we would be moving. We were joining the large Southern migration north in search of jobs, opportunities, and a better life. I couldn't have been more pleased. I was always ready to go to a new place and experience different things. Savannah would forever be part of me, but when Big Momma said we were moving to New York, I was ready to do cartwheels. Nothing and no place was as exciting as New York City! Tall apartment buildings, subway trains, the finest clothes, and tons of people - for a small-town girl like me, New York sounded like heaven. I couldn't wait. Big Momma went ahead first to set up house. Everyone else went to Washington, D.C. where my father had a brother. I didn't mind going back to Washington. It was only temporary.

Uncle Jim and Aunt Min lived right across from Howard University. Even though they weren't college folk, they took great pride in being near what many considered the best colored institution of higher learning in the country. They were both retired and remembered a time when colored folk had no such place to point to. Howard sat up high on a hill making sure the entire city took notice. I even held up my head and stood tall when I glanced across the street.

Uncle Jim liked to nip at the bottle. Aunt Min would send him to the store for a loaf of bread and he wouldn't come back until two weeks later. Sometimes Aunt Min would be upset, she'd wonder if anything had happened to him, other times she'd just be plain old mad because she knew he was out spending his little money on liquor.

The family usually let one or two medical students stay in the house. It brought in a little extra cash and gave these future doctors a cheap place to live. We didn't see much of them though; they were always rushing down the hill to Freedman's Hospital. And when we did see them, we wished they would go right back to medical school. They used long words that none of us could pronounce, and talked about different types of germs that were everywhere. They brought home parts of bodies and tried to keep other weird things in the refrigerator. They used to want to sterilize things in my aunt's pots, parts of bodies and skeletons, stuff like that. The thought of eating something from a pot that had had a dead part in it was too much for me. It was disgusting. I tried to stay out of their way as best I could.

⟨⟩

Even though she was in the grave, my allegiance remained with *my* mother. As I got older, however, I understood that Daddy Pops needed love and affection too from a companion of his choosing. My stepmother provided that. She was a lovely woman who favored my own mother. She made my father happy and brought back his quick smile and easy laugh. We all needed that. I tried to be grateful.

Times were tough what with our move and starting over. Everybody who could helped out. My stepmother was no exception. She worked at the Bureau of Engraving while my father worked at some sort of shoe factory. Daddy Pops was the packingest man around. I mean he could out-pack most women, including Big Momma. Alonso, my eldest brother, from my mother's first marriage, was a talented artist. He was also unusually quiet. When you greeted him in the hallway, he would just grunt. Clearly he had other things on his mind, but he worked painting signs and brought a little more money into the household. Like the other men in the family, he felt a duty to work hard and help support the household. He really was talented and could have done great things in the art world.

I really don't remember how I felt when my stepmother became pregnant. I know I wasn't too keen on sharing my father with yet another person. My mind was focused on getting out of the school and hopefully doing it without embarrassing my family too much. Back then, unlike today, the reputation of the family was important and had to be considered before you did something too crazy. I also had to plan my grand entrance to New York.

When my stepmother and her unborn child died, I felt no deep sense of emotional loss. I had not bonded with her. Somehow, traveling to and from her job at the Bureau, and working in the drafty old government buildings which lacked central heating, my stepmother contracted pneumonia. Once again my father became a widower.

The pain I did feel was for my father who had to suffer through such loss again. With my own mother, in between two of us, there had been one stillborn child. Daddy Pops seemed to shrink a few inches after my stepmother's death. Even at my young age, I could see that his smile was like that of a clown, painted on and temporary. Only God knows how he managed to hold on. I mourned for him.

I soothed myself by listening to a few tunes on the phonograph. The records at home were stale and too formal, but I played them anyway, humming and swaying as I tried to figure out my next move. Visits home, even over the summer, were too short. Before I knew it, it was time to go back to school. After my celebrated freedom at home, I was even more rambunctious at school.

Frankly, I don't know how Holy Providence tolerated me as long as it did. One afternoon, I convinced a friend named Celina to sneak out of the dorm with me. We tiptoed up the hill to the barn near where the nuns lived and scooped up a baby pig. The fact that we weren't supposed to be there just added to the excitement. I decided that we would roast it. One of us carried matches. We walked around and gathered twigs and branches to make a fire. The grassy hill with trees to one side provided the perfect cover. I had never cooked anything in my life, but I wasn't going to let that stop me from roasting this pig. Nor did we have any idea that it needed to be butchered and gutted beforehand.

It probably didn't take much for the nuns to discover something was wrong. The pig was squealing loudly and nothing we said or did would shut it up. By the time they actually got to us though, we had a pretty good fire going. I don't know what we would have done next if the nuns hadn't shown up. But when they did, we took off running down the grassy hill toward the school, the pig grunting and snorting the whole time. As they chased us, they seemed to float across the grass, their winged habits and full skirts propelling them forward in hot pursuit. They looked like human flying penguins. Finally they caught up with us and took our piglet away.

I didn't see what the big deal was. After all, I hadn't actually cooked the pig. Its life had been spared. Wouldn't this God that the nuns were always talking about forgive me? Funny, even though I clearly intended to cook that pig and I would have found a way to do it if God hadn't intervened, when they snatched the piglet out of my hands, I felt just like I had back home in Savannah, when Big Momma got rid of my pets.

I escaped that place by telling them that I had to go home to convert my father so he would get into heaven. I thought they would love that one. But Sister Mercedes called Fredi in and told her that I had an imagination the orphanage could not handle. Based on my behavior, they felt I would be much happier at home.

At the end of the school year, Fredi went directly to New York. I couldn't wait to follow in her footsteps. Big Momma thought it would be best for me to live with her so she could control me. I didn't argue because all I wanted was to be in New York, all glamour and excitement.

CHAPTER 6

Slicing the Big Apple

When we finally moved to New York in 1919, the Great War had just ended. People call it World War I now but we called it the Great War because we never imagined that there could be one larger, more violent, and with even greater loss of life. Black soldiers came back from France talking about how "free" they had been and expecting more of the same right here at home. The *New York Daily News* first came out that year too. They had plenty to report on and people searched the paper for stories on the war and the economy. Even though we usually couldn't afford the paper, we could always read the headlines. They were constantly full of exciting things to talk about. That's how most of us got the news back then. Reading the newspaper was one of the few diversions we had.

We hoped things would get back to normal, if there was a normal for New York City now that the war was over. Everything in the city seemed so cool and expensive. We weren't dirt poor, but we didn't have a lot of money either. What we did have was a lot of mouths to feed as my father began to expand our family with his third wife, Gertrude. At first we stayed with Daddy Pops and our new stepmother on 129th Street, but then we moved in with Big Momma in a railroad apartment on 135th and Eighth Avenue. Each room was right behind the other off a long narrow hallway. I was twelve years old, still innocent but not shy by any means. I was very curious about this fascinating new place.

My relationship with my second stepmother, my father's third wife, was good. We lived in New York City, the most exciting place in the world, and I had my own life. I was less worried about my father's affairs. Daddy Pops and his wife moved to Queens, they got a house out there. Whenever I went to visit, my stepmother would make me tongue and cabbage. I loved it so. I wouldn't eat it from anyone else's kitchen, but she made it for me special. I could see that she was good for him and that he was happy. I began to call her mother. When she became pregnant, I was glad for both of them. They had four children together: Trudy, Juanita, Floyd, and James. We were one large happy family. We treated all of the siblings the same.

Daddy Pops had a car but he preferred to ride his bicycle. The car was for the boys. One of the last Christmases I was out there, we all got him a new bicycle. It had a great big red ribbon on it. We were sitting in the kitchen having breakfast; it was fairly early in the morning. The door was closed because Daddy hadn't come down yet. We were sitting and talking when in rode Daddy Pops on his bicycle saying a jolly "Merry Christmas!" to all of us. He would have killed any of us for riding the bicycle indoors, but he came rolling in like Santa Claus himself.

Even though our family was big, and space was always something there was never enough of, these few rooms had far less square footage than we were accustomed to squeezing into. Rosebud stayed with Daddy Pops so we wouldn't overload Big Momma. Whenever we were over at Daddy Pop's place, he'd remind us "to keep the man out of his pocket" when we left a light or something on. Everything in the big city was expensive including electricity.

Our apartment was on the top floor of a six-story building. I'll never forget the location of that place because it was near a police precinct where I was later arrested. I'm sure it must have tired Big Momma out climbing up and down all those stairs, but she could still lay a good one on you when she wanted to. Fortunately, we had outgrown Dr. Black Pill, who had retired. What we hadn't outgrown was the church. Big Momma found a Baptist place she liked nearby. And no sooner had we gotten halfway settled in than Fredi started talking about church too. Not just any church mind you, she was talking about Mass.

When Fredi shook my shoulders early one Sunday morning, I tried to ignore her.

"Bel, Bel, wake up, it's time to get ready for Mass," she said.

"No, I'm not going," I yawned, my eyes still closed.

"Get out of that bed, you're going to church," she ordered, almost sounding like one of the nuns back at Holy Providence. She went into the bathroom and I put the covers over my head. When she came back into the room we shared, she yanked the covers off of me, catching one of my kid curlers in the blanket.

"You are going to church, so you'd better get up now," she said, in her raised eyebrow tone with her arms crossed. My deep breath ended in a pout and I knew she wouldn't leave me alone, so I got up. I moved real slow using the only power I had.

Even after putting on my plaid Gingham dress and my black Mary Janes with the strap across the instep, I tried my one last excuse.

"But my hair," I said turning away from Sister in the narrow room.

"That's what hats are for," she said, plopping a cotton hat on top of my head that covered my curlers.

When she grabbed my arm and headed for the door, I didn't pull back too much. She was the oldest girl, and what she said went. Besides, we were already late.

At church, there was only room in the back pews. Sitting on the hard dark bench, I dangled my feet, stared at people's outfits, and silently thanked God for escaping pinafore prison. If I had to be at Mass, Mass in New York City was better than Mass anywhere else. Besides, I still had to avoid becoming a heathen and church was the only way, I reminded myself. It wasn't so bad after all.

After the Pope blessed the Italian flag that went over to Ethiopia with the Italian army to kill people, Fredi became disgusted with the Catholic Church. She said, "It's time to go!" and she meant it. We walked out and never have gone back. Far too many people died in the name of religion which was supposed to be about life and how to live it better. I didn't miss the church at all. The city had so many other things to occupy my time.

Everywhere I went, I paid close attention to the swank New York accent. At school I practiced the accent until I thought I sounded like a native. Then I practiced some more. If that's how the stage wanted me to talk, I would be ready. I studied my lessons with no great interest in any subject. I have never had a great interest in academics. Performing was my only dream. After school, Fredi and I helped Daddy Pops at Black Swan Records. He was the head packer for shipping. We sat at these long narrow tables in a big room. In between licking stamps and sealing envelopes, we talked about the latest records coming out. Sometimes we practiced our favorite songs on each other.

Black Swan was the first black record company. The whole industry was still in its infancy, but white companies wouldn't record blacks. When they did record black songs, they were sung by whites. It was the same thing with the movies from that time period. If there was a role for a light-skinned black person, chances are it was played by a white person. That way, they could avoid any of the racial mixing whites seemed to be so terrified of. It also kept the roles we played to minor ones. But the mood in the country was changing. The smell of opportunity was in the air. Black Swan was set up to ride that magic carpet. Harry Herbert Pace and W.C. Handy set up Black Swan so blacks could begin to meet our own needs. Pace named the company after a wonderful singer who was called the black swan because of her beautiful brown complexion and lovely voice.

While I kept my eye on the stage and performing, it didn't take long for economic circumstances to cut Fredi's education short. She tried to finish up at Richmond High School, but at sixteen she was legal to work, and we needed the money, bad. Her first job was in a stockroom of a dress house. It paid a whopping $17.00 weekly. That really was a lot of money back then. In those days most people went to a tailor or seamstress and had their clothes made. Very few people could afford to go to department stores and buy off-the-rack clothes.

I really admired Fredi. She was so in control, so much of an adult. I sat at my table at Black Swan licking sticky stamps waiting to follow in her footsteps. After she got a little experience under her belt at the dress shop, the record company hired her on as a bookkeeper. They paid her a little more too. Then she heard about her next job while still at Black Swan. That was the one that would change our lives forever.

Fredi heard about an audition for a part in a Broadway musical. She wasn't that interested. But when she heard how much it paid, $35.00 a week, she changed her mind. With no prior experience, she auditioned for Elida Webb, the choreographer, and was hired for the chorus of *Shuffle Along*. Sister was ecstatic and we felt like we had won the lottery. Making that much money she could almost take care of the household by herself. This all-black musical took New York by storm, not only because of its zany dances like the Charleston, but also because of its portrayal of black love. The writing, the music, the dancing, everything was done by colored people. Several of the songs from the production like *"I'm Just Wild About Harry"* and *"Love Will Find A Way"* were hugely popular and are still celebrated today.

Now Sister's only worry was to find the words to tell Big Momma and Daddy Pops that she would be dancing on stage with half her clothes off. No one had to tell us that nice respectable girls didn't gyrate and kick up their heels on stage in skimpy costumes. But this was Harlem in the twenties. Nothing was as exciting as the stage. Once the family got over the shock of Fredi's jump into show business, they actually surprised us. Big Momma said, "If you do it, make something of it." Fredi told her not to worry. I held my breath and let Fredi speak for the two of us. To Big Momma, as long as we kept our virginity, carried ourselves properly, and acted like the ladies she raised us to be, it was okay to make a living dancing. Fredi and I both had minds of our own, but we also craved and needed Big Momma's approval.

Shuffle Along was a fabulous success! It ran from 1922 until 1924. Florence Mills was the star and the dancing was literally out of this world. Sister traveled with the show. She said it was hard, painful, exhausting work sometimes, but the stage sounded like nothing but fun to me.

Maude Russell was also in the show with Fredi. She was tall and slender, with a pretty face, and a dancer's body. She could make us laugh no matter the circumstance. She befriended Sister when Fredi needed some help. Fredi got into the show, but she didn't know how to make up her face. Dancers didn't have their own make-up artists. Maude took Fredi aside and showed her the ropes. I met Maude shortly after Fredi and we began to forge a close friendship. She had such a fabulous sense of humor and really enjoyed having fun like me that we became easy friends. I got to practice making up my face until I got pretty good at it.

As Fredi rehearsed until she thought a limb might fall off, another star was being born right along side her, Josephine Baker. *Shuffle Along* was a first for both of them. A lot of the girls didn't like Josephine. Most of the showgirls were fair-skinned with sharp features. It didn't hurt if you had wavy hair either. They thought Josephine was too dark and too ugly to be in the show. They thought she acted silly. One time, in the dressing-room, they threw out all of her make-up. Fredi made them go back and pick it up. I started to understand a lot more about the power of light skin and how much we as a people hated part of ourselves. The only people complaining about Josephine Baker were what we called "high yella" girls. And those calling members of the cast, like my sister, out of their names were darker skinned. It seemed like you couldn't win on either side.

Fredi knew that no matter how fair a person was, in the eyes of a white person, they were still colored, and therefore not equal. She taught me this valuable lesson which is part of the reason why I continue to describe myself as colored. The labels may change on the outside, but what people think in their hearts, that doesn't often change with the name. Fredi was called some unflattering names herself by other dancers but of course she could handle herself so the name calling didn't last very long.

While Fredi sashayed in sexy exotic costumes, I licked

stamps and waited impatiently for my opportunity to dive into show business. Sometimes I sang to help the time pass. My whole body itched to get into show business. The bright lights sparkled in my eyes, the gorgeous costumes and shoes mesmerized me, and I couldn't wait to get all that attention.

When a man who worked for the record company heard me singing my favorite song, he told me that I had a very pretty voice. I sang in a high-pitched thin voice, imitating the popular singers of the day like Florence Mills. I was trying to be proper and elegant. To my surprise, the man turned out to be Fletcher Henderson, a writer for Black Swan Records and a popular Big Band leader. He liked my voice so much that he put together two songs for me that were recorded in 1923 - "I Want to Go" and "That's Why I'm Loving You." In my teenage eyes, my singing ability proved that I belonged in show business. Even my sister didn't sing. Now I burned to dance and act, just like Fredi. When she auditioned with no experience, she told the choreographer if other girls could do it, she could too. I felt the same way; if my sister could do it, so could I.

On my way home, I passed Bess and Co., one of the finest department stores in the city on Fifth Avenue. I had already made my first record and I thought I was somebody because I could sing. I'm telling you this money I received had already burned a hole right through my pocket. I saw this gorgeous pair of baby blue Mary Janes in the store window. They were leather with a cross strap across the instep. Oh my God, they were so pretty. I went upstairs to the Shoe Department. The shoes were sitting on a table with a drape falling on either side. I picked them up. The sales girl walked up to me and asked if she could help me.

I said, "Yes, I like these shoes!"

Now I only had thirty-five dollars. I thought about the money. I thought I was a millionaire when I got it, but buying the shoes would mean spending all I had. I looked at the shoes and thought about the money, squeezing it in my pocket.

"Okay, I'll take them," I said.

I went home with the shoes. I didn't even have money for the bus so I walked. When I got there I was scared to go upstairs to Big Momma because if we made money we were supposed to bring it home to her. We lived at the top of a building on 135th Street. Every time I pass 135th, I think of that apartment on the top floor. I walked up the steps to the roof top and hid my shoes up there, but I knew she was going to ask me about the money. So I told her I had bought a pair of shoes.

She said, "You did? Without asking me?"

I told her that I had seen them and they were so very pretty.

"And how much did you pay for them?" she asked, the unavoidable question. So I told her.

She screamed at me, "Get those shoes!" Her voice shook my body and I knew I was in big trouble. She took them away from me for what seemed like a very long time. It was maybe a month. Then she brought them back and called me in.

"I'm going to give you these shoes. You spent your money. You made the money. I'm going to let you have them. And you can wear them." I'll never forget that day. I had been so angry and mad at her for taking my shoes, *my* shoes! But that day all was forgiven. She just didn't understand, when I saw those shoes, I just had to have them. I ignored the fact that I had been selfish and impulsive and only thinking about myself when the family was barely getting by, but I felt that I deserved those shoes. If Fredi had done what I did, there would not have been food on the table for us to eat.

I was on cloud nine when she gave me my shoes back. Walking down the street, I would stop and turn my foot and look at the shoes. I'd sit down on the curb and look at my shoes. Boy, was I happy. On that day, not even heaven would have made me any happier than I was already. Everybody that came along, I showed them my shoes.

From the very first time she got a job on stage, Fredi tried to persuade me not to go into show business. She thought the life was too rough for me. She was too late. At home, I glanced at the clock on the kitchen stove - half past. It was time to go. Listening carefully to make sure Big Momma was fully occupied in the kitchen, I gently cracked open the front door and tiptoed down the first landing. I didn't have to bother to lock the door. As I ran down the other five flights, my pounding chest wouldn't let me consider the beating I might get when I got back. All I could think about was getting to the theater at 62nd and Broadway before the curtain rose.

I headed for the side entrance of the Colonial Theater. They let me in - one of the benefits of having a big sister already in the business who was working in another show. I stood in the aisle just to the side of the stage where I could see and hear everything. Singing along with every number, I practiced the moves, imitating the performers on stage until I just about had the whole show down pat. Backstage I talked to the dancers, singers, and comedians, hoping they would drop a useful tidbit that might help me get into the show.

"The show is great. I would love to be in it," I said, giving my best stage grin.

"We'd love to have you," was the usual reply.

Each and every time I attended a rehearsal, which was at least twice a week, I received nothing but encouragement. As the show neared opening day, I remained excited but began to lose hope about actually performing. At the very next rehearsal, during one of the breaks, the director asked me if I wanted to be in the show. One of the girls in a quartet, Revela Hughes, had come down with laryngitis. I was so happy I forgot to feel bad for the woman. Of course I wanted to be in the show! I knew the part and I was ready. My fate was sealed. After that I was put in as her understudy.

Running Wild opened during the week of September 21st, 1924. Thanks to a birthday in May, I was now legal to work. We performed several times a week, including matinees on Wednesday and Saturday. Great seats were about $2.00. Thursdays were my favorite; there was a show at midnight. Not only did I get to stay up late, I got to perform in front of all those people. After the show I would be so tired and sleepy that I'd practically fall asleep in the taxi home. But I'd force my eyes open, just so I could inhale another breath of New York air. I was hooked after my very first performance. I knew what I had been born to do and one way or the other I would make my way in this show business arena.

The town was really something back then, even without all the skyscrapers and the Empire State Building, and before it became a piece of fruit. To me, New York was, is, and always will be the most exciting town on earth. I just couldn't get enough. Humph, it was some of the things we did in the twenties and thirties that made New York shiny, red, and delicious.

CHAPTER 7

Cotton Under My Toes

"The little drama queen" - that's what everyone in the family called me. Considering how much I loved acting, I really couldn't disagree with the label too much. Just when I started feeling good about my natural-born talent, I would hear Little Momma's voice.

"Chile, your tear ducts are next to your bladder!" she would say, shaking her head in disbelief, as though I hadn't inherited my talent directly from her. As long as my thunderstorm tears stopped them from tearing up my bottom, I didn't too much care what they called me. What mattered most was becoming a star and receiving earthquake applause so loud that it would cause temporary deafness.

It was the beginning of the rest of my life when I cut that record for Black Swan and performed on stage in *Running Wild*. Now I was Isabelle Washington, not Fredi's little sister. Changing the spelling of my name gave me my own identity and made me feel special. Now, no sacrifice would be too great. Most of the cast for *Running Wild* had come from *Shuffle Along* when Noble Sissle and Eubie Blake had parted ways. Most of them were experienced professionals and I was part of the cast. I could not believe it!

The Harlem of the 1920's was far more than an after-dark amusement park; it was an intoxicating roller-coaster ride that kept us coming back for more. We thought the fun would never end, that the park would never close. The Cotton Club and Connie's Inn were the cat's meow of the day. The gams that crossed those stages resembled champagne bottles of the finest labels, and belonged to some of the prettiest, most talented, "high yella" girls who made their way to Harlem. They were top of the line establishments, with doormen, beautiful women, and all the liquor you could pay for. Only light-skinned girls were permitted to dance at these higher end clubs. The country had a confused sense of beauty that excluded so many beautiful and talented darker-skinned sisters who never had the same opportunity. Don't get me wrong, we knew we looked good. We worked hard to shock the audience and even the other girls with what we dared to wear, the more risqué the better. And you could not tell us that we weren't gorgeous in whatever revealing costume we wore. We had twenty-inch waists, petite figures, and perfect make-up. But excluding the Josephine Bakers of the world was just plain wrong.

Many of the girls like myself and Fredi had no formal training. We were naturals determined to slink our way to success. We didn't care what it took. However many hours practicing to get the moves just right, we would do it. Having ambition and wanting to be famous was not a crime, but being too dark in the field of entertainment was a serious offense. Other colored people were real quick to point the finger too. It went way beyond a complaint from another dancer in the chorus line. Theaters had people called spotters. It was typically their job to "spot" colored people who were trying to "pass" or enjoy something set aside for whites. The spotter would go up to them, apologize, and tell them they had to leave. They would be escorted out. Just the thought of a spotter was enough to make me ill. If whites wanted to preserve the race, then they had better move to another planet. People jumped back and forth across the color line at will. Whites had better just get used to it. Harlem was a thin weak line that would break sooner or later.

Even the famous Cotton Club practiced its segregation but so much. The place got its name from a band. It used to be owned by a Jack Johnson and it carried his name then, but when someone came in and performed with his Cotton Pickin Band, the name stuck and it became known as the Cotton Club.

My start at Connie's Inn came from Fletcher Henderson; one of the band leader's that I had made a record for at Black Swan. The Seventh Avenue bus would drop me at my stop shortly before midnight. There would already be a smile on my face. 131st Street was just a short walk up the way. Nodding my head and greeting a few strangers along the way, I would pull my sweater around me a little tighter and pick up my pace. Connie's Inn was right next to the Lafayette Theater. I would take the side entrance and head straight back to the dressing room in the corner.

The room was a medium-sized rectangle divided into left and right, but united by a long narrow mirror along the full length of the wall. As various dancers arrived, simultaneous conversations swirled around the room about who would be singing that night, how good we looked, and which speakeasies people planned to go to after work. I took off my clothes and slipped into the costume waiting behind the high-backed chair where we sat painting on perfect faces of pleasure with our own make-up.

The wardrobe woman helped me tuck everything in just so. I had to be especially careful with the plastic breast pads I wore up top to enhance my meager endowment lest they fall out while I was on stage and turn a sexy exotic strut into a comedy review. I looked in the mirror and smiled at myself. Damn, I looked good. I had done well that day, had hardly drank any water at all. When I first started dancing, a more experienced girl told me not to drink water if I wanted to stay slender. It sounded like good advice at the time.

All of us were ready well before the five-minute advance cue. We stood there for the few moments waiting to go on, reciting the chorus girl anthem in our heads, "Turn your palms out, shoulders back, and tuck your tookie." Then we strutted out on that dance floor like it was nobody's business, showing everybody that we were born to dance.

Our entrance was greeted with a roaring silence, fixed stares, heavy cigar smoke and the smell of home-brewed gin. From the moment we walked out on the floor, two hundred eyes tried to undress us. They didn't have to work very hard with the costumes we wore. The sound of breath being taken away chased the nervousness from the pit of my stomach. I looked over their heads at the empty space and focused on the sweet rhythms the band put out. The white linen-covered tables surrounding the U-shaped dance floor created an obstacle course for waiters carrying plates of food and drinks. While some patrons hovered over the small round tables taking an occasional swig from bottles they brought in themselves, which the management allowed as long as they were discreet, others sat back deep in their chairs trying to get the best view of the show.

The well-to-do customers on the edge of the floor were literally close enough to reach out and touch us. But that was strictly forbidden. Not just because we were performing, but because we were colored dancers in a room full of whites. All the staff was colored, from the doorman and waiters, to the wardrobe woman and cook, but the clientele, and Connie and George Immerman, the owners, were white. Like prohibition, the law has never stopped people from doing what they really wanted. Whites came to the club to experience the tame side of coloredness from a good safe distance. We made sure they got their money's worth.

In the era of Billie Holliday's strange fruit, people flocked to Harlem to taste its exotic forbidden fruit. While we danced in all-white clubs, colored men were still being lynched. As we gyrated and kicked up our heels in establishments we could not patronize as customers, Jim Crow laid down the law. Even if we had been allowed to go in, only a few of us would have been able to afford the exorbitant price of admission. As unemployment inched skyward, and the street became home for so many people, we had a way out. Each week when I saw my check, I sighed with relief. A roof over my head and food to eat, I knew how lucky I was.

The harsher people's circumstances became, the more Harlem seemed to thrive. Blacks couldn't go to the higher-end white clubs but they flocked to places like Hoofer's Club in Harlem, one of the places Bojangles hung out. There were a number of places where people just about inhaled jazz, blues, and poetry. And there was always a rent party going on somewhere. We'd pay anywhere from a dime to a dollar to get in. The bathtub would be full of some homemade concoction, and anywhere colored people went there was always food. At the rent parties we let our hair down. White people didn't need to see that side of us so they weren't invited.

We would all have a good time jumping and swaying to the music and somebody's rent would get paid on time. Colored people earned the least of any group, but that didn't stop the Harlem landlords from charging some of the highest rents in the city. That's why there were so many rent parties. Our apartments gave us a dry place to sleep during the harsh New York winters.

After work, my best friend, Maude and I started up a little business. We'd serve light meals, like soup, to the other dancers. Of course, I had lots of help from Big Momma because I really couldn't cook to save my life and Maude wasn't much better. After the soup, if we weren't too tired, we'd head to an after-hours place for the house specialty, fried chicken and waffles. Then we'd head home for a good day's rest.

In no time at all, I left the chorus line and became a soubrette doing specialty numbers. We performed five nights a week, at midnight and two o'clock in the morning. Generally a show included a black-face comic routine, a top-line singer like Florence Mills or Ethel Waters, the chorus line dancers, and special routines. At intermission, the band would take a break and people would dance to recordings. In between shows, we took our meals in the dressing-room. For the most part we ate whatever we wanted, just not too much. When one of us even looked like we were thinking about putting on weight, somebody would give her that look. At a time when most people didn't get enough to eat, we had it too good to risk losing all this over a few mouthfuls. By this time we were making one hundred dollars a week, a virtual fortune.

One night I put on my glittery silver costume. It was a one-piece strapless suit with a little bra at the top and very little covering my behind. I danced behind a thin sheer veil with a dim blue light creating the mood. I spread my toes on the smooth wooden floor and swayed my hips to the mid tempo band music. When the drummer tapped his stick, I pressed my body forward and shook my hips. Staying in one spot, I turned around slowly so everyone could get a good look. With my arms in the air, I tilted my shoulders from left to right and swirled my body slowly. I was maybe ten minutes into my snake dance when a bunch of police came rushing into the place.

"This is a raid," they shouted through one of those loud bull-horns, setting off a mass of confusion. People were trying to get out of their way as fast as greased lightning. The band stopped playing. My heart was pounding. People were shouting and cursing. I didn't know what to do, and tried to move, but where could I go dressed like this? The police came and got me. How would I explain this to Big Momma and Daddy Pops? They threw some kind of blanket around me. Mr. Immerman whispered to me on the way out the door, "Don't giv'em your real name."

I sat in the back of the police car next to an officer while the other officer drove us to the precinct. When they asked my name, I made up something and gave them the correct spelling. They wrote something down at the station, arrested me for immoral dancing, held me a short while, and let me go. The next night I did my snake dance again, uninterrupted. I guess whatever payoff had been made to the appropriate person.

After nearly two years at Connie's Inn, the only place to go was the Cotton Club, the hottest spot in Harlem. Long shiny black limousines competed for the best street parking. It was built on a big rock on Lenox Avenue and sat way up high on 142nd Street. The front entrance was guarded by a uniformed doorman who wore a cap and navy blue suit with tails covered in shiny brass buttons. The waiters dressed exclusively in black suits with ties. And only the very best of the best could dance and perform there.

Climbing up the several flights of stairs to the dressing-room above the dance floor was a workout in itself. But now that I was a soubrette, I shared a room only with other principal dancers. There were mirrors on all of the walls and we had our own wardrobe woman.

Downstairs on the main floor, the band covered the entire back wall of the dance floor. Unless dancing feet were laying out new steps on the floor, customers sat back, faced the band, and let themselves be hypnotized by the hot tunes floating up from the back of the room. Small round tables seating at most four persons dotted the room.

After all the jumping and jiving of the earlier acts, me and my dance partner sort of calmed the place down. Roger held me in his arms nightly for nearly three years. Tall, graceful, and very handsome, he wore black satin pants and a crisp white shirt. Midway through the show, we would walk out on the floor and dance a fairytale. I wore an off the shoulder chiffon dress with delicate straps and a full skirt. It would twirl out nice and full when he turned me around. He placed his hand on my waist as though I were fine china. Then he would swing me out and roll me back into his chest as though I were his most prized possession.

We were only out on that floor for a few minutes each night. I tried not to notice that most of the customers were good and drunk by then. Some of them could barely keep their heads from drooping. They didn't care that I was a living Cinderella waltzing around the floor with my prince. I had to find a way to bring his dream to life.

I fell in love with the fairytale my partner and I created on the floor. I knew I wanted a man who could make me feel like that all the time. The applause was meager. Maybe they didn't even realize our number was over. Mr. Starks, the owner, stopped me as I came off the dance floor. I knew what he wanted. The same thing he wanted the night before, and the night before that - for me to sit and talk with some man who wanted to meet me. This man came to the club so often; he began to blend into the paint on the wall.

"Mr. Starks, I'm really busy tonight," I said, looking to the stairs I would have to climb to get to the dressing-room.

"This man is E-X-T-R-E-M-E-L-Y wealthy. You can have A-N-Y-T-H-I-N-G you want. You know how much you like nice things." Mr. Starks tried to convince me to meet this man, but I wasn't having it.

"Well, I'm very sorry, but I just can't meet him tonight."

"Isabelle, the man just wants to meet you, to sit down and talk with you." Mr. Starks put a little more insistence in his voice.

"Not tonight. Maybe another time," I shook my head and moved passed him.

What did he want with me? No matter how fair my skin was, I was still colored. Couldn't he find a white woman to give his attentions to? I could not be bothered. Maybe he wanted to take his little safe fantasy a bit further. Well, not with me he wouldn't. I just wasn't raised that way.

The man who ran the Cotton Club was nuts about Fredi. He would constantly proposition her. We knew many of these people who provided us with employment were gangsters so there was no way either Fredi or I would get involved with them.

Outside I stepped right into a waiting cab. My body fell onto the seat like luggage. I took off my shoes and began to rub my feet. The plump black leather helped me to relax as I thought about what excuse I'd give Mr. Starks tomorrow.

The next night Mr. Starks was even more insistent. Finally he asked me to do this for him as a favor. I gave in. After the show, once I had changed clothes and put on my make-up, I went downstairs and approached a table right on the edge of the dance floor. The man was well dressed in a nice suit. He stood up when he took my hand. Mr. Starks looked over at us from across the room and smiled. When he turned his back, his shoulders dropped, like a heavy weight had been lifted.

"It's so nice to meet you," the man said smiling.

"Nice to meet you too," I said, nodding with only a corner smile. We sat across from each other. I crossed my legs and sat up straight, letting my shoulders relax down.

"You're quite a lovely lady," he said, looking me straight in the eye. I thanked him for the compliment and looked away.

"And you're such a beautiful dancer," he said, turning his head to one side. "I've come here so many times just to see you dance. I would like to take you out some time, if you'll go out with me," he continued, seeming just a little bit nervous.

"Thanks for all your kind words. But I can't go out with you. I just can't do that."

"Why not?" he asked, making me nervous.

"I'm just not interested," I replied looking past him. "Sir, it's getting late and I have to get home."

"Can I give you a lift?"

"No thanks, there's a cab waiting for me now."

"Thanks for meeting me. I'll be here if you change your mind."

"Thank you sir, but that's very unlikely."

CHAPTER 8

The Glass Eye

Showgirls were always beautifully dressed and extremely popular. Anywhere we went, people gawked at us like celebrities. Guys would make passes at us. We tended to go out in groups. For a while Spanish shawls were quite fashionable. We would put those over our clothes, dressed to the nines, and strut like nobody's business.

As a happy-go-lucky showgirl who was crazy about life, I had one thing on my mind. Preston Webster had other ideas. By the time we met, I was already at the Cotton Club. He was tall, fair-skinned, and handsome, but it was his sparkling glass eye that I fell head over heels for. Preston was a photographer extraordinaire, and he kept taking my picture. That clunky box he lugged around let him see things that I never imagined. Like a bird staring at the big picture, he was able to zoom in on the little things that made something really special. Unlike so many other men, when *he* told me I was beautiful, I believed him. As he had me pose, I imagined myself on stage, except I couldn't shimmie when he pulled the switch. He kept snapping my picture until the camera blinded my eyes.

Preston had a little D.C. in him, but like everybody else, he ran to New York when he got the chance. After practicing his craft under the hands of George Scurlock, "the" photographer for colored people, he left his reputation in the nation's capital and came to the city armed with his mechanical eye. Backrack's on Fifth Avenue liked the view. So did I. When we married a short while later, I was barely more than a teenager at eighteen. I thought I was set for life walking down the aisle in Big Momma's church. He was about twenty-five.

I knew nothing about contraception. Neither Big Momma nor Fredi had explained the facts of life to me. There were some things that we just didn't talk about back then. I don't know how they expected us to know these things when no one ever told us. I learned more about sex from the Cotton Club girls than I did from my family.

Preston and I found our own little apartment on McCoombs Place in Harlem and settled in quickly, because the baby was on the way. I felt so grown up. My family was happy and relieved. They predicted that marriage and motherhood would have a calming effect on their little drama queen. I was thrilled about the idea of having a child, but I was also scared; scared that the mirror wouldn't recognize my body afterward, that my clothes would no longer let me in, and that I just wouldn't be able to dance any more. Show business and kids didn't mix well. I had to keep my figure. While I knew my headstrong determination was critical in this industry, I also knew that my complexion, hair, and nice figure were just as equally important.

Well before my son was born, Preston and I headed back to Washington, D.C. Howard University trained most of the country's colored doctors, and Freedman's Hospital was right down the street from my aunt and uncle. I remembered that my mother had lost a child and my first step-mother had died with child. I didn't worry quite as much having the finest doctors available to me right there.

One thing that I was very fond of in Washington, D.C. was going down to the waterfront and getting seafood. I loved going over there in the open air and buying fresh fish. The market reminded me just a little bit of Savannah. I would get some type of white fish, take it home, and fry it or bake it. Fish with a bowl of rice would always do me good. I couldn't cook well but I could make do with fish and rice.

The baby came in November of 1925. I was just eighteen. There were no complications and I thanked God for my healthy baby son, Preston Jr. Afterwards, my stomach flattened out, leaving my twenty-inch waist intact, and I went right back to the stage. I had a loving husband, an adorable child, and a fabulous career. I left like nothing could stop me. Motherhood didn't have to ruin my life. I never even thought about staying home. Preston thought otherwise. It wasn't so much that I worked as what I did to earn a living. He didn't want his wife, the mother of his son, strutting her stuff around stage in front of other men. To him there was no artistic value at all in what I did.

Now I know that show people didn't have the best reputations back in the twenties and thirties. Some were even downright scandalous, but a few of us did know how to conduct ourselves. Why, in my entire life, I've only had about six boyfriends. I think that's pretty good for someone approaching the century mark. When I met Preston I was a dancer, it's what made me happy. I didn't see why I should stop now. When we were dating, one of the things he liked about me was that I knew how to have a good time. Was I supposed to change who I was? Having a husband and a son didn't mean that I could no longer have any fun.

At the time, most women stayed home after they had children. Those that didn't may have wanted to. I was making a decent income but the country was inching toward the depression. People were already on the street starving. I had never ever wanted to be a housewife. After a while, Preston made it clear that he wanted me to stop working. I'm sure it bothered him that he couldn't come into the club and see the show. As a colored man he couldn't patronize the club.

I tried to ignore Preston. Instead of staying home, I took my baby to work with me. I can still see the little tot playing on the blanket with his toys in the small dressing-room. He was so innocent and happy. He would look up with a big smile on his little face when I came back into the room. I wouldn't say this to the patrons who used to frequent the place, but of all the males at the Cotton Club, I do believe my son Preston was the darling of all the girls. They used to compete to baby-sit him. They took good care of him so I didn't worry so much while I was dancing. When I finished my set, I packed up my baby and took a taxi home.

Don't get me wrong, I loved my husband. He took good care of us. He put up with my many faults for years. I still don't understand how he managed not to starve to death, cause God knows I could not cook. Not knowing your way around the kitchen was not the kind of thing a woman could admit in mixed company. Big Momma helped us a lot. And Rosebud babysat and helped out a bunch too. But the attention, applause, and adoration from the customers was intoxicating, maybe even a little addictive. Despite being Preston's wife, I was still a woman, a very young and attractive woman. And I was living my life's dream. As a young person with your whole life ahead of you, you never think it will end, the accolades, the praise, the fun, but the curtain does come down, eventually. I couldn't stop, not for a man, not even to save my marriage.

One night I came home so exhausted that I didn't bother to have anything to eat. I dropped my things, prepared a bottle for the baby, put him to sleep and crawled into bed next to Preston. The next morning we woke up to pitiful calls of "momma." When we glanced over at the crib to check on the baby, I nearly screamed. He was in black face like the sambo comedy acts. We raced and got the poor thing cleaned up. All I could do was thank God that he hadn't swallowed any of the stuff. Black shoe polish was smudged all over him; there was even a bit on his tongue.

Once I knew Preston Jr. was okay, I really had to chuckle. He had seen me apply make-up with a powder puff and had watched girls at the club get ready for the stage. I would have to tell them about this one. We never left anything on the nightstand after that. And if this was the baby's way of suggesting that he might try to follow in my footsteps, he had another thing coming. He would go to college and make something of himself. Preston used the incident as proof that I should stay home and mind the baby. What he had to say just led to another argument. Why was it wrong for a woman to continue working after she got married and had a child?

I think most women in Harlem worked if they could find a job. Harlem was really something back then, in the twenties. You didn't dare go out without putting on your best outfit. You never knew who you might run into. Men with neatly trimmed hair slicked back tipped their hats and made way when you were walking down the street. They opened doors and waited for you to pass in front of them. Poets gave our feelings voice. Colored performers danced, acted, and sang in numbers never before seen. The Duke, Louis Armstrong, and others did things to music that almost made the dead tap their feet. Historians call it the Harlem Renaissance. I call it life. Child, I was living right in the middle of the cat's meow, and Preston wanted me to keep quiet and be still. It was too much to ask. I felt like he was trying to smother my life up under his. For the first time I began to have reservations about my marriage.

When he became more insistent that I quit working, I refused. He couldn't see that it was only him that I loved, but I needed the stage too. It gave me a high like no other, a harmless fix. One night he got angry and began a shouting match. My stomach was in knots and the baby started to cry. I just looked over at my husband and shook my head. Soon I would have to leave to go to work. He wouldn't hear of it. We were both surprised when he struck me. I hollered out and fell back onto the couch. He looked at me and then stared at his hands. I didn't say a word through my sniffles. I was too small to fight him. But I made up my mind. If another man ever hit me, he'd better not go to sleep. I would boil water and pour it scalding hot down his ear. No one else would hurt me.

I packed a bag, grabbed Preston Jr., took some of his things, and went to Big Momma's. I hoped she wouldn't make her usual prophesy when something bad happened - that the world was coming to an end. I couldn't listen to that kind of talk tonight. I loved Big Momma dearly, but she was elderly, and had used up most of her years. I was young, full of life, with many years to come. Maybe she was tired of saying it, or maybe she knew I just couldn't handle it at the time, but that day that I went groveling back to her house, she did not condemn the world. Nor did she condemn me. Instead she embraced us and welcomed us home. I was ever so grateful.

I became physically ill over my marital woes. I didn't see any way out and so I resigned myself to not think about our future together. Preston wanted me to come back. He promised never to lay a hand on me again. I couldn't take that chance; I had a son to raise. Preston got more depressed than usual. He begged me to come back. He couldn't live without me. I thought about the smack on the face and the make-up I had to use to cover it up and the excuses I had to give for the next several days until the bruises healed. I refused to give in.

There was nothing for me to be ashamed of. This break up was his fault, not mine. Lots of the girls slept with directors and producers and whoever to get parts. I hadn't done that. At night I came right home. Even though all of the dancers were light-skinned and pretty as a picture, there were girls waiting in line to take our places. All I ever wanted was to make people happy. What was so wrong with that?

Shortly after I left my husband, I found that I was pregnant again. I couldn't believe it. It couldn't have happened at a worse time. It was difficult enough to take care of one child, let alone two. Surely it would ruin my career. I had only just barely gotten back into the club scene, the life that I adored and wanted to continue forever. I could not do this by myself and I could not do this with Preston. I just couldn't go through this again with him. No woman should have to bear children for a man who beats her. I was determined not to.

I went to talk to Maude, my close friend, she would understand. She was older, wiser, and more experienced. She had had an abortion and lived through it. Lots of showgirls did, because babies and show business didn't mix well together. So many of us had been taken advantage of. All we wanted was to be stars, for the bright lights to focus on us and for the applause to never end. It didn't even cross my mind that abortion was illegal. How could the law tell me what to do with *my* body? I had to do what was best for me, best for all of us right now before it was too late.

Me and Maude went to the drug store but I didn't know if I could actually go through with it. We got the powder. My situation was desperate. I thought about little Preston Jr. and how happy he was. Yes, he should be the only one. When I lost the baby, I wasn't too surprised but it still hurt. I told myself that it was for the best. Maude assured me that everything would be all right.

By the time we divorced, Preston was in a bad way. I didn't even want to leave him alone with his son. I didn't know what he would do. He took some time off and went to Canada. He used to like to go skiing up there. The fresh air and beautiful views usually cleared his head and made him feel better. I was somewhat relieved when he left.

At least I would have a little while to think about this whole mess. Each day that passed, I was convinced that I had done the right thing. He was in a beautiful place clearing his head. We would figure this all out when he got back. Then we got the news. Preston was dead! No! I just couldn't believe it. It couldn't be. There must be some kind of mistake. He was just here. My shock turned into guilt because of how we had parted, but there was nothing I could do now. How could he do that to himself, to us? I closed my eyes and thought of my son, who looked just like his father. What a tragedy to be fated to grow up without a father. Then I remembered the smack. All of the deep love I felt for my husband left in that moment. I refused to let myself be emotionally torn over Preston's choices.

Preston's body was brought back to Washington, D.C. His family wanted the baby to come and pay his respects. I didn't feel right about going myself under the circumstances. And I wasn't so sure that seeing his father lying in a pine box was the best thing for my son. So neither of us went. My precious little baby was only about five years old; about the same age I was when I lost Little Momma. I knew how traumatic that had been and thought it best not to put my son through that.

How could we get over the shock of losing him like that? It wasn't just his life. He was part of a family. He had a son. He had no right... I know his family blamed me, but it wasn't my fault. Sometimes I could barely get out of bed. I thought the tears would never dry up. What had I done to deserve this? Little Preston was an innocent child. My life was a mess. And each day the boy looked more and more like his father. My career and my baby were all I had. Throwing myself into my career was the only way I was able to keep going. Not only was I a divorcee, I also had a son to raise. We didn't use the term single parent back then. Divorce was synonymous with scandal and of course the wife was blamed even when it wasn't her fault. Thank goodness my family was there for me. Dancing and taking care of my baby made me feel almost like a whole person. That was my life. Now, I had to keep going for his sake.

I didn't need another man who would be just like Preston. Maybe I didn't need a man at all. I had a son. But my son needed a father. I couldn't imagine ever falling in love again, getting married again. I'd probably never meet anyone anyway. After taking care of the baby and working, I was so exhausted that I knew I wouldn't have time for anyone else, even myself. Raising my one son was more than enough for me to handle. Now that I was a parent myself, I wondered how Big Momma and Daddy Pops raised the five of us.

CHAPTER 9

Why I Don't Eat Broccoli

Harlem was hotter than the little red nigger peppers my father grew in the backyard in Savannah. He'd let them sit in vinegar with a little salt for a month or so before he'd use them. Then I'd shake the bottle over my hominy grits at breakfast. That's where I got my taste for hot. So I was ready for Harlem. The smoke hovering over the clubs signaled to everybody that Harlem was the place to be. I tell you, you can't possibly know what heaven is on this side of the divide until you receive outrageous applause from hundreds of complete strangers who adore your every move. I kicked up my heels and smiled on cue with all the other dancers, but I kept my eyes on Broadway. That's where the real stars glittered.

My first stop on Broadway was *Harlem*. The play was all the rage to whites but only a few colored had come to see us. Colored folk thought there was too much sex and partying in the play. Debauchery they called it. After a few scenes were deleted everybody came to see it. I played a foolish young girl who takes off with a numbers runner, hangs out at rent parties, and basically goes wild. A wonderful woman named Ellen played my aunt in the show. I couldn't believe it when I found out she was Roger's mother. Roger had been my dance partner at the Cotton Club. Always smooth on his toes, and a quick study when we had to learn a new number, now I saw where he got both his good looks and talent from. We got along fabulously.

"I'm the hinkley Cordelia," I said, strutting out on that stage as my soft blue dress with ruffled trim swayed with my hips. The matching tam cocked to one side of my head gave me the hippest look in town. Except for my gum carrying on its own monologue, there was nearly complete silence. But it only took a New York minute for the audience to get its tongue back. Harlem had become so popular that Broadway had taken notice. It couldn't get much better than that. Harlem was so hot that Broadway actually did a play about Harlem. We couldn't believe it.

Every night at the end of the show, I fell deeper in love. Staring over a sea of heads, the lights blinding my eyes, I wrapped myself in the audience's embrace and lost myself in the sound of appreciation. Finally, after several minutes of clapping, the entire cast took a bow. I left the stage with a deep grin on my face. I had done well, had given them my very best. When the room full of smiling faces left the building, I couldn't have been more pleased.

Backstage, chatter and laughter hit me from every corner. It was impossible to follow the various conversations. Pride was etched onto our faces. Somebody was talking about going to get something to eat. Another group was heading uptown to Harlem to go clubbing. I wanted to go anywhere but home. I was just too excited and needed to celebrate. I caught Ellen's eye and went over to her for a victory hug. Not only did New York like our play, we were actually a hit on Broadway! I was hooked. I wanted it to go on forever. In the dressing-room, I washed off my make-up and replaced my ruffled skyline and tam on the rack. My face looked like it belonged to a sad clown.

Ellen came over to me. All we could do was smile at each other.

"Say, why don't you come over and spend the night at my place. I'm only a few blocks away and we have a show tomorrow afternoon." I nodded and smiled my agreement. We could fall asleep talking about the show, and then get up and do it again. Perfect.

Early the next morning there was a knock at the door. I was on my second cup of coffee. A man walked through the door looking like he had come from a concentration camp. Ellen called for Roger to come down. He introduced me to his friend, who sat down to have a bite to eat. His name was Adam. He was tall, with smooth straight dark hair, gangly, and light skinned. He was definitely easy on the eyes, but I really didn't take too much notice of him.

No sooner had he sat down than we had to get ready to go. The theater was only two blocks away. Adam asked if he could walk with us. We didn't mind but decided to take a cab the two short blocks. I didn't want to say it, but the man should have stayed at the house and had some breakfast. He was so hungry looking.

"Can I ride along?" he asked.

"Sure," I said, not waiting for Ellen to respond. She looked over at me and I gave her my sly smile. Adam walked around to the other side of the car.

In the car, we talked about the show and how excited we were to be on Broadway.

"Can I come see you some time in the show?" Adam asked, as he helped us out of the car.

"If you like," I smiled just being polite, not thinking anything of him.

He did come down though, to the show - while he was still in town on Easter vacation. He sent a note backstage and asked if he could stop by. I was surprised to see him again. This time he didn't look so desperate for a meal. And he was a friend of Roger's, so of course I had to be nice to him. A short while later, I received a letter with a return address from Colgate University. Adam asked if he could call me Bunny Girl. I wrote him back saying yes, if I could call him Bunny Boy. Why should he have all the fun? I never looked at the Easter Bunny quite the same after that. The long-eared fluffy bunny transformed itself from a floppy cartoon character to my symbol of love and happiness.

The thin, lanky, fair-skinned college boy who looked like he needed a good Thanksgiving meal slowly became a tall handsome prince who took my breath away. Even though he was miles away, he touched me all the time. Just knowing the postman had run was enough to get my heart racing. Checking the mail became a daily treat, better than chocolate or ice cream, that kept my cheeks flushed. I told myself that he must really be learning something up at that school because his words did a number on me. I took extra care responding to each handwritten envelope.

After several letters back and forth, he wrote saying he'd be back in town soon. I ran through the rest of the page. School was fine, but he couldn't wait to get back to the city - to see me. And yes, he wanted to take me to dinner! I reread that line several times, until it hit me that I would actually be seeing him again. We would be going out, on a date, alone. I had to decide what to wear, how to fix my hair, and whether to go high or low heel.

I was so excited when he actually returned that I was afraid I might say something really dumb or commit some faux pas that would turn him away forever. On the night of our date, the meticulous care I took in putting myself together just so didn't seem to matter at all; I never even got to eat dinner. Just being near him was more than enough. I paid close attention to his every word. Like any gentleman he was properly dressed in a suit and tie when he came to escort me out. He was so handsome and charming; I just couldn't get over it. And I, like a lady, wore a conservative but fitted outfit which showed off my legs, with gloves and a pocketbook. My gloves came up only to the wrist; we called them "shorties." I didn't want to be too formal with him. He seemed like so much fun.

We were seated in a downtown restaurant on the East Side off of 42nd Street near the train station, one of his favorites. No one had to tell me that this was a high-class restaurant. I followed his lead and ordered steak, though my appetite was not for food. I hadn't really dated anyone since the death of Preston. Even though he was gone, I still felt an odd allegiance to his memory. It didn't make sense that I could be developing feelings for someone when Preston was barely cold in the grave. I reminded myself that even if he were here, I wouldn't take him back. I had to relax and enjoy the evening. How often would a fellow like Adam take out someone like me?

We were just a few sips into our drink when the waiter brought our plates out. Adam looked over at me, smiled, and nodded his head as he began to tear into his steak. I reached for my knife and looked down at the plate. The room felt kind of warm. My stomach tightened.

"Bunny, this is delicious," he said, shaking his head and smiling. "How's yours?"

I tried to swallow, so I could speak, but my voice was trapped somewhere down in my gut. I reached for the water glass but I couldn't pick it up.

"What's the matter?" he asked, his voice full of concern.

All I could do was stare down at the plate. I took a quick breath and forced myself to swallow so I wouldn't throw up.

"Ugh!" he said, with a frown, pressing his lips down.

A large fat worm, the same brilliant color as my former favorite vegetable, was resting comfortably on my broccoli. My body was paralyzed. I turned away from the table. Thank God Adam was there. He clapped his hands loudly, calling the waiter immediately. The white manager came out red-faced, obviously worried about the reputation of his establishment. The waiter zipped our plates away and apologized at least ten times. Other people began to look over. It was embarrassing. I didn't want them to think we had done anything. The waiter asked if I'd like something else. I said no, nothing. Adam helped me stand and got me out of there lickety split. Of course, we didn't have to pay and the next meal would be on the house. If there ever was a next time.

Adam wanted to take me somewhere else, but after that incident, the only place I wanted to go was home. Any appetite I had was now long gone. Adam kept apologizing and told me nothing like that had ever happened in all the years he had been going there.

By the time he got me home, I had calmed down a bit. I was actually able to smile. I said goodnight to Adam, he helped me out of the car, and I went upstairs. So much for a romantic evening.

Flo Ziegfield, a big name on Broadway, had come to see me in *Harlem*. He was crazy about my acting but wanted to see if I could sing. There was a part for a mulatto girl who sat on a piano and sang "*My Bill*". He made an appointment for me to come to his theater. I was so excited about the possibility of another role on Broadway that I practically forgot about the worm. Of all things, it would have had to have been a worm, the slimy crawly things I hated the most. Just for a moment I was back in Savannah. Bubba was chasing me as I ran and screamed while looking back every now and then to see if he was gaining on me. Bubba would have loved to have pulled the broccoli one on me at the table. He would get a real kick out of hearing this one.

Several days later, after I had fully recovered from the worm episode, I let Adam take me out again. We went out a number of times after that. He wanted to expose me to everything in his world. Fascinated, I was an eager and willing student. We had even gone riding at a place on Hudson River Drive several times. They had an old horse named Rose that was just my speed, slow. Today we were headed to the Yale Club. I was so excited that he thought I was ready for this. Adam truly loved horses, and now he wanted to share that love with me. He brought me a blue Yale T-shirt to match the one he was wearing. He really wanted to teach me how to horseback ride. I paid close attention to his instruction but my heart was beating so loudly that I was barely able to follow along.

Adam kept reminding me of previous riding trips and how well I had done. He knew we would have a ball. It was so much fun to ride. By the time we got to the Club, I had almost convinced myself he was right. His words were reassuring and I was determined to be brave. There was no reason why I couldn't learn to ride a horse well. I would do it.

While we waited for the horses, he carefully explained how I should handle the animal. He took my hand and looked me in the eyes.

"Do not be afraid. They can sense fear. I'll be right here with you the whole time. Remember you've done this before. It'll be just like riding Rose." Rose was an old horse who was more like a pony than the hoofed beast in front of me. She belonged to Adam's aunt. I had very serious second thoughts as my heart kept pounding, but I couldn't find the words to tell Adam no.

He gave me a kiss on the cheek. I felt better but not confident enough to ride the horse. My heart was pounding so loudly when he helped me climb up on that massive thing, I'm surprised he didn't hear it. Maybe the horse did. The tail kept swooshing all around like it had a life of its own. I was definitely scared. I kept my eyes on Adam as he mounted his horse with no effort at all. He made it look so easy. I couldn't remember a single thing he had told me to do. All I could do was watch and follow.

"Okay, Bunny, now I'm just going to go ahead of you and lead you. Hold the reins like this and your horse will follow mine." It was supposed to go into a trot but it had other things on its mind.

I grabbed the reins just the way he instructed and did exactly what he told me to do, but the horse wouldn't mind. It started neighing real loud and reared up, pressing its front legs toward the sky. When I saw how big its teeth were I thought it might try to bite me. I think it was telling me to get off its back. It didn't care how light I was. I barely had time to scream as it threw me to the ground with a loud thud. I wanted to run away from the monster, but my foot was caught in the stirrup. Before Adam could calm the thing down, it had dragged me several feet. I was in such pain, my back felt like it had been cracked open. Even the groans from my throat hurt and the tears burned down my face. Adam came running, but he was already too late.

"Bunny, are you okay?" Adam kept asking.

He tried to help me up. I held out my arm to say no. That monster stood there towering like it hadn't done anything wrong. Adam moved the beast away. I couldn't believe this was happening to me. The pain running down my back wouldn't let me move. My back hurt worse than when I was in the delivery room. My clothes were smeared in dirt and horse manure, and my own blood. The smell made me nauseous. I couldn't even imagine what a sight I must be to Adam, the one person in this world I wanted to impress most.

The woman at the front desk was very apologetic. She didn't say anything when we left. She had given us more spirited horses because she thought we played polo. Maybe wearing the Yale shirts wasn't such a good idea. I ended up with a cast over half of my body. I couldn't work and I couldn't get around too well either. I needed help just to take care of my son.

Adam had to go back to school. He felt just terrible about the whole incident. Fortunately I had Big Momma and the rest of my family. Everyone chipped in to help take care of the "invalid." I was in that thing for weeks. I had to have all of my clothes altered and cut to fit the cast. Slowly the pain began to dull, but it never went away entirely. I also began to have female problems. The pain would leave for a while and then come back for frequent visits. My back has bothered me in one way or another ever since.

After the accident, there were even more calls, and visits, and gifts from Adam. I told him a number of times that it wasn't his fault. He kept apologizing and bringing me presents. We spent more and more time together. There was no mistaking that Adam and I both fell hard. We really hadn't expected this. He took me to dinner and shows. He surprised me with flowers because he thought they could learn something about beauty from me. And almost every weekend, he came to New York City from his college in up state to see me. Sometimes he would bring an extra suitcase and I would have one of my friends behind the bar give him some booze.

Colgate had an annual winter carnival in February. Adam came home to Harlem to get some black girls. I was his date. We had such a great time. I hadn't laughed so hard in years. Adam wasn't the only comic; I had him in tears with a few of my own jokes. I went to visit him too a few times at school when I didn't have professional engagements. He wanted me to see and know all parts of his world, the world that he wanted to share with me.

One weekend Adam was in town, he took me to a soiree. When we got hungry we headed over to the food table. He started feeding me something. Just having him directing a fork at my mouth was enough to make me try anything. Whatever it was, it was really good. I grabbed the fork out of his hand, finished the dish and asked for more. He asked me if I liked it. "Ump Hump!" I nodded my head. It was so good. When he told me it was chitlings, I could have died. It looked nothing like those nasty pork parts hanging in the butcher's shop, along with pig tails and other parts. I grabbed my stomach saying, "Oh, no." But it was too late. I had already eaten them and had even had seconds. I had told him that I didn't like chitlings and that I didn't eat them. He teased me about it afterwards. It's one of the dishes that I learned to make later.

Coming from the South, everybody feels that you eat pig feet, pig tails, chitlings, and hog maw, but we never ate that kind of thing at home. I learned to eat all of that with the Powells. We would go down on Eighth Avenue, there's a meat place down there. For New Years, we'd get a case of pig feet and three ten-pound tins of chitlings because Old Man Powell and Adam, they loved them. They taught me and Preston to eat them. Mother Powell would stand there and clean those things, the chitlings, all the guts and stuff, and she'd cook 'em real good, but she never even tasted them. She wouldn't eat them, but she taught me how to clean them and cook them so that I could make them just as well as she could.

As I began to spend more time with Adam, I also saw more of his mother. Mother Powell was an absolutely wonderful woman.

She took me under her wing and taught me her baking secrets and special recipes. She had lost a daughter, Adam's sister, and I think she missed the kitchen talk that women engage in. The butter for a cake should be at a certain temperature and whipped only so much. Adam liked his steak just so, it's not to be overcooked. She taught me things that you can only learn from an older woman, the kind who has a son who sees the way he looks at you and how happy he is. She was truly a blessing to me.

1. Early picture of the Washington children. From left to right: Fredi, Alonso, Isabel, and Robert (Bubba)

2. Fredi, Rosebud and Isabel with their billy goat and cart

3. Robert Washington (Isabel's father) and Sarah Washington (Isabel's grandmother).

4. Washington family home in Savannah, GA

70

5. The Washington Sisters
Fredi, Rosebud, and Isabel as
three little Indians

6. Big Momma (Ella Brown) out
shopping in New York, 1934

7. Young Fredi and Isabel in school uniforms at convent in Cornwell Heights, PA

8. A teenage Isabel with a violin

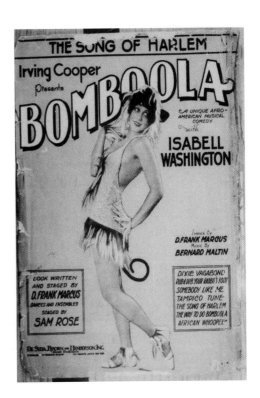

9. Isabel as a star in Irving Cooper's Bomboola in 1929

10. Isabel as a show girl in the 1930's.

11. Fredi and Isabel as angels at Christmas pageant in Cornwell Heights

12. Alonso as a Captain in the 369th Infantry Regiment (Harlem Hellfighters) New York National Guard in the 1920's

The Romance Gets O.K. of Deacon Board

MISS ISABELLE WASHINGTON
an intimate pose snapped in her dressing room at the Hippodrome Theatre upon her last visit to Baltimore. The Deacon Board of the Abyssinian Baptist Church has approved the romance between her and the Rev. A. Clayton Powell, assistant pastor. This approval removes a barrier to their marriage.

REV. A. CLAYTON POWELL, JR.

13. Isabel and Adam at time of their wedding announcement in 1933. (Isabel Washington Powell Papers, Amistad Research Center at Tulane University)

14. Isabel preparing to sing hits from Bamboola during the evening Journal Sports Hour, 6:00pm. WPAP. (Isabel Washington Powell Papers, Amistad Research Center at Tulane University)

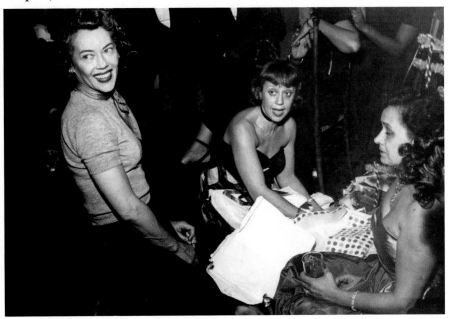

15. Fredi, Isabel and a another sister (Jenny) at New Year's party in 1939.

16. Isabel and Adam at the Bunny Cottage in 1930's.

17. Isabel and Father Powell

18. Fredi and Mother Powell

19. Washington family photo with young Preston behind the camera. Adam and Isabel are on the right and Mrs. Valentine is between Preston and Adam.

77

20. Fannie Robinson, Isabel, Adam, Fredi, and Bill Robinson at 20th Century Fox after completion of "One Mile From Heaven" - 1938

21. Isabel making a great catch of a 12 pound blowfish, 1935

22. Isabel and Adam

23. Adam showing his fishing prowess, 1939

24. Isabel posing while on vacation in Martha's Vineyard

25. Adam on the beach at Gay Head

26. Friends and Isabel at right on running board of a Packard

27. Isabel with a whopper catch

28. Preston in his Navy uniform, and Isabel in 1945.

29. Preston, Isabel and friends on the beach July 27, 1953

30. Isabel and Adam

31. Wingy and helper at the Bunny Cottage

32. Ruby Dee, Fredi, and Ozzie Davis with Dr. Merritt Smith and his wife

33. Fredi and Isabel in their later years

34. Preston, Police Chief J. Carter and Isabel in Oak Bluffs

35. Isabel and grandson Tommy

36. Isabel assisting one of her special needs students

37. President Clinton and Isabel

38. Isabel relaxing on front porch

CHAPTER 10

Love Will Find A Way

When Adam invited me to his church, I had to shush the little Catholic schoolgirl buried inside me. I knew he was a preacher's son, but I just hadn't thought about going to church. Even Sister fought with me about God's house. I didn't want to go with her, and I wasn't too sure I wanted to go with him either. When he saw that I couldn't decide, he turned to face me.

"Abyssinia is the largest, wealthiest black church in the country. You'll be right at home in Harlem," he said, gesturing with his face like you know what I mean.

"You'll love it, and it'll be good for you." Now he was using the voice that told me he knew what was best for me.

"Besides my father can preach. He just might save your soul."

We both had a good laugh over that one. It would take a lot more than a fire and brimstone message from Old Man Powell to save me. The thought of sitting in church next to my Bunny Boy while his father tried to preach the devil out of me was enough to make me go. I knew the man didn't care for me. It wasn't me so much as the fact that I was courting his son, his only son, who he had plans for to take over the church. He liked to remind me that showgirls and church folk didn't belong in the same family. I didn't worry too much about him though; I had Adam's complete and undivided attention. As determined as Old Man Powell was to break us up, Adam was set on us being together. Like father, like son.

I looked at this tall handsome preacher-to-be, thought about how wonderful he had been the last twelve months or so, and decided to give God another try. As much as I had tried to avoid the Heavenly Father, back in Savannah, at Holy Providence, and even here in Harlem, He had pursued me and wouldn't let go. Maybe it was time to give in. For the first time since we'd been dating, I had to stop and wonder if Adam just might be serious about our relationship.

Adam took me to exhibits at the Metropolitan Museum of Art. While we stared at the works of the masters, he held my arm and explained about the history of the paintings. We went horseback riding in Connecticut so many times that I became good friends with his Aunt who lived in New Haven. She was a talented seamstress who made the most gorgeous dresses and gowns. We strolled through Central Park holding hands and sneaking kisses behind trees. He constantly bought me the most beautiful flowers.

We ate dinner at the best restaurants all over New York, and most of them did not serve worm-covered broccoli. He came to several of my shows, and every time I turned around, he had a present for me. He even gave me two grammar books, <u>Pitfalls in English</u> and <u>Putnam's Phrase Book</u>. He didn't want me to be embarrassed, no matter how fancy the people were who came around. You see, some of the church members and others who knew Adam thought I wasn't good enough for him. I didn't go to finishing school or anything like that. And back then very few women went to college. They stayed home, kept house, and minded the children. Adam wanted me to be ready for the snobs who thought he should have done better. He wanted to be as proud of me as I was of him. No other man had ever been so good to me. I wondered how long it would last.

While Adam was stealing my heart, God and I continued to work out our differences. I was at the church so much, the parishioners must have thought Adam and I were joined at the lips. My routine became Old Man Powell's evening service, Mrs. Powell's late supper, then off to work at the Cotton Club well before the midnight show. The audience must have wondered what kind of juice I was on. All they saw was me walking on air. My feet never touched the floor.

In my heart I was saying that I have a real life Prince Charming who is so wonderful that I know we'll live happily ever after. Sometimes Adam came and watched me perform. At the Cotton Club the people were so close to the stage, it was all I could do not to rush over to him, sit on his lap, and wrap my arms around him. Of course, I had to show off a little when Bunny Boy was there. I strutted across that stage, shook my fanny until it almost fell off, and kicked up my heels all the way to the sky like there was no tomorrow. Even though he was colored, Adam had no problem getting into the club because of his fair skin and he was well to do.

Old Man Powell seemed to loosen up too. Or maybe he just got used to me being around. I spent hours in the kitchen watching Mrs. Powell chop, taste, and bake. Everything she made was wonderful. I was thrilled when she started explaining her cooking secrets to me. I didn't know what a chitlin was before I went into her kitchen. She taught me how to clean out the guts and doo doo and cook' em up real good. Some of the things a girl learns from her mother, I learned from Mrs. Powell. I was grateful. She took to me much sooner than her husband. She was more concerned about the happiness of her son than anything else. Me and Mrs. Powell, we had a lot in common. We both wanted nothing more than to make Adam the happiest man in the world.

I worked hard to fulfill my end of the bargain. I studied the church and tried to master every element that would help me fit in better. I attended church regularly and discussed the Bible with Adam and others. Sometimes I practiced what I would say ahead of time to make sure it came out properly. At one of the services, I turned my head and saw someone who looked kind of familiar, but I couldn't place the face. It was my childhood friend from Washington, D.C., Elyse White. Of course she was all grown up and married now. She had a family of her own. Unlike me, she had stuck to the books and was now a school teacher. It was so good to see her, especially now. She might be able to explain how I could get on people's good side here at Abyssinia. She was a member. What a blessing to run into her.

When Adam found out she knew me from childhood, he acted like he had hit the jackpot. He gave her his best smile, turned up the charm a notch, and asked her how I was when I was younger. Then just like that, he asked how old I was? He said he couldn't get a straight answer out of me. My standard response was that a lady doesn't tell her age. He looked over at Elyse with a question mark on his face and his eyes wide. I gave her a look and explained that Elyse had been my teacher back in D.C. and was older than me. It became our little joke, but Elyse never gave me away.

Everything in my life seemed to be coming together quite nicely. I absolutely loved my work. I was courting the man of my dreams. His mother and I adored each other and were getting close. And I was learning how to fish, one of Adam's favorite activities.

Fishing is something that always put a smile on Adam's face. He learned it from his father and went every chance he got. I think Adam liked to fish even more than horseback riding, and he certainly loved horses. The family took me out fishing several times. Even Mother Powell used to fish, but it was actually Old Man Powell who taught me. Once we got past the worm part which I couldn't stomach, I took to fishing pretty well. I learned how to cast my line and hold it just so to attract more than a little bite. After a while I began to look forward to fishing as much as Adam.

My brother, Bubba, used to come fishing with us as well. Like Adam he loved to fish. We would go to Florida or some other spot, but Adam liked the island of Martha's Vineyard best. We would go up to the bridge late at night, maybe around midnight. That's where the striped bass would be chasing the minnows. Our lines would be in the water and we would be waiting with anticipation just knowing that we were going to get lucky. It was usually dark so we had to make sure our lines didn't get crossed. Before we knew it, a fish would be flopping in the water. "They're biting," someone would say and everybody would get excited, but we had to keep our excitement down so we didn't scare away the fish.

Catching the bass was tricky because they don't have teeth so we couldn't always feel a tug on the line. But when we heard them flopping on the water, we knew we'd made a catch. We couldn't always see them too good either because it was dark, so we learned how to listen real good. When Bubba would catch a great big whopper of a fish, he'd yell out, "Shit Molly with the green neck tie!" Those things weigh up to about fifty pounds. We'd tell him to shush and then we'd all start laughing. There's something very special about fishing at night under the stars.

Martha's Vineyard is good for bass and porgies, my fish. That white fish is so flaky and tasty; I could eat it every day. If we weren't pulling in the one, we'd go out on the boat early in the morning and look for the other. The boat would be rocking and there was generally a chill in the air. We wouldn't talk much, at least not until the first catch. Then me or Mother Powell would talk about how we were going to cook the fish.

"I'm going to add a little salt and pepper and fry it in cornmeal," was my usual comment. At the table I would add a little hot sauce and I'm never without collard greens. Adam liked his the same way. I only felt a little sorry for the fish every now and then. While they were preparing for their last supper, I would be thinking about the good eating I'd be sitting down to. The porgies were much smaller fish than the bass so I didn't have any problem pulling them off the hook. I tell you, fishing may be one of the quietest activities, but it's also one of the most exciting. We usually caught more than we could eat so we would take the extra and sell it to the fish market.

I saw a fisherman decapitate a swordfish once. It was a

grisly sight with the guts spilling out and the shiny eye staring up. I watched anyhow, thinking it might make me less squeamish. Besides, I liked a good swordfish, and if I could eat them, I should be able to clean them. When I stepped up a little closer, I saw what looked like worms in the fish's head. "What's that?" I asked him. "Oh, that's nothing. These maggots grow in the head of the swordfish," he told me without giving it a second thought. Maybe it was nothing to him, but it was truly disgusting to me. From that day until this, I have never eaten another swordfish. After seeing that, I decided that cleaning chitlings is easy compared to fish.

I performed in a bunch of shows on and off Broadway, but Old Man Powell was a far better actor than me. He had us all duped into believing he could accept me. We found out the truth when Adam told his father about his plans for our future together. The old man nearly lost his mind. There was no way his son was going to waste his time with a showgirl. I was not the right *type* of woman for him. He didn't understand why Adam couldn't see this for himself.

Old Man Powell was madder than hell. He thought he knew just the right thing to bring Adam back to his good senses. The Old Man took his son before the Deacon Board. Of course the Old Man did all the talking. The Board could block Adam from becoming the church's next pastor, the job Adam was born for. I guess Old Man Powell didn't realize how much Adam was like him. After his father spoke, the Board agreed with him that a future pastor should not be dating a showgirl. Adam stood before them all without fear and told all those holy men in suits if he couldn't have his Bunny Girl, he didn't want the church.

I'm sure the Board was surprised, probably mad enough to spit fire. And Old Man Powell likely had a conniption fit. The Old Man expected the Board to do the right thing, to set Adam straight. But he had also hoped that Adam would listen to them. Everyone knew that having Adam as the next pastor was the best thing for the church. He was young, handsome, well educated, dripping in charm, and helping people in distress was in his soul. The membership simply adored him. Reluctantly, the Board did what was best for everybody; they let Adam have his Bunny Girl.

I was absolutely thrilled when he told me how he had stood up to them. I felt vindicated. How dare they suggest that I wasn't good enough. I didn't know what I had done to deserve this kind of love and commitment. Adam risked losing the thing he wanted most so he could have me. From this point on, it was clear to me that Adam felt the same way about me I felt about him. We would love each other forever, come what may. I could not have been any happier. But now I would have to have a close talk with God. His house didn't seem so bad anymore. I would have to give Him and His house a try.

It was fortunate that we didn't have to put our back up plan into action. If Adam wasn't going to be at the church, we considered eloping. When we got back, he would give lectures and I would sing. Adam attracted people like honey. He could fill up a hall with no problem. And I was a Broadway star with a tiny waist and a sweet voice. Somehow we would make it work. His father could keep his money and the church could keep its closed mind.

My work at the club helped me take my mind off of worries at the church. It should have been the other way around. But I stood right by Adam's side. He had made the right choice. Even so, when someone told me about an audition for another Broadway play, I got just a little excited. They were looking for a certain type, so I was lucky to even be considered for the role. I practiced a few songs to warm up my voice, then I went for my audition. I was scared. This was for Flo Ziegfield; he was tops in Broadway at the time. He was a short thickset man who looked like he knew what he wanted. I was so intimidated,

He told me, "Now little lady, don't be scared."
I sang in a light-airy-full high voice. It sounded beautiful to me. I backed myself into the piano, rested my elbows there and belted it out. I starred into space to avoid looking at his face. Before I got all the way through the song, he said, "Great," and told me I had the part.

"You mean I have the part, really!" I had to repeat it because I could hardly believe it.

He was laughing and smiling. All I could do was put my hand to my mouth. He shook my hand.

"Oh, thank you, thank you, Thank You!" This was one of the greatest honors!

I couldn't wait to tell Adam. Starring in a Broadway show - the part of Julie in *Showboat*, well, what would he think of his Bunny Girl then? Would his father finally accept me as the professional entertainer I was, and not some floozy? I had to hurry up and get home with my heavy good news. Ziegfield later commented, "Her voice belts out like a whistle at high noon." He was talking about me!

When I told Sister, she gave me a big hug, shook her head, and stood back to take a good look at me.

"My little sister. It seems like just yesterday you were running from Big Momma and Dr. Black Pill, now you're starring on Broadway! Come here!" "Momma would be so proud of you.

You know I'm proud of you!"

As I ran over to see Adam, I told myself if I died tonight I would not have missed anything! Over at the parsonage, Adam was in a good mood. The church was working out the details of the transfer to him. I thought I would burst with my news. After a hug and kiss I just had to tell him.

"Adam, remember I told you I had an audition coming up, well it was today."

He just looked at me and grinned.

"I had to sing, not dance," I said, looking him in the face, knowing what he was thinking.

"And I got the part!"

"You got the part," he said in a kind of flat tone. He was only half smiling. And I knew something was wrong. Maybe something had happened at the church, something about the transfer. He would tell me sooner or later, but I couldn't let his news spoil mine.

"So, what do you think I should do?" I asked, just knowing he would give me the answer I expected.

"Don't take the part." He was talking real slow. I knew I must have heard him wrong. I repeated his words to myself and waited for him to correct himself.

"Because then we'll never be married. You know preachers and showgirls don't belong in the same family, Bunny Girl."

I had to swallow, so my voice would work. "Oh, Bunny Boy!" I jumped up into his arms.

"Oh, my God." He held onto me tight. My feet were dangling in the air. My tear ducts started to flow, but these were tears of sheer joy. I didn't have a care in the world. Both of us were moaning. I thought winning the part on Broadway was the most wonderful thing in the world. But this, becoming Mrs. Adam Clayton Powell Jr. was even better. I must have died and gone to heaven. No, this was better than heaven. It was real life. Mine.

All I could think about was becoming Mrs. Adam Clayton Powell! I went to church regularly and tried to conform to the conservative environment at Abyssinia. I stopped wearing the fancy glamorous clothes of dancers and toned my dress down. I smiled and tried to be extra polite to the members so they would like me. But there was one woman in the church who hated me no matter what I did. She would stare at me some kind of crazy. I sat with the deaconesses up front and at the side of the church. She usually managed to sit nearby. I would smile and nod my head but her constant staring began to make me very uncomfortable.

During the holiday season, the church was always beautifully decorated and there was a Christmas tree downstairs in the church where the young people's services were held. This woman hung a little box of toy blocks on the tree one year with Adam's name on it. That's when we began to suspect that she was really going out of her mind.

She appeared at church wearing the same clothes and hats that I wore. I knew something was very wrong. The men in the church loved to dress like Adam in their linen suits and different outfits that Adam was fond of, but women just don't do that. You want to stand out a little from your neighbor, to be noticed, feel special. But this woman would go to my dressmaker and milliner and have the exact same dresses and hats made. She studied how I carried myself and tried to imitate me in every way. When she actually did speak to me, we could hardly believe what she said. Like the Lindbergh kidnapping, she was going to climb up a ladder and steal me. She was desperate to get me out of the way. She figured that she should be the one to be with Adam. We went to the police. They told us to be very careful of her because the woman was mentally deranged. They warned us that she might even try to throw acid in my face.

The woman continued to attend services. She was there every Sunday and made sure that I saw her. When I tried to keep my distance, she would inch closer. One Sunday morning, the head of the Federation of AME churches, a white minister, spoke at Abyssinia. He gave a wonderful sermon and when service was over, he and Adam and several of the elders remained in the pulpit talking. Members were remarking on how good the message was and some were waiting to meet the visiting minister and shake hands with Adam. I was headed their way so I could shake the man's hand too.

All of a sudden, this woman jumped up, left the pew, ran over to me, and struck me hard in the ribs. I doubled over in pain and let out a yell, turning heads all over the church. When Adam saw what had happened, he jumped down from the pulpit several feet above the main floor of the congregation. The woman dashed out and headed for the downstairs exit. Adam and some of the others managed to trap her in a ring around the rosie circle.

The police came and took her to Bellevue Hospital. They kept her there for a couple of days for evaluation. She was in a huge room with nothing else but a pail of water, a running faucet, and a mop. In those days I learned that this is one of the first tests they give people to see if they are sane. They brought us down to observe her. I watched in disbelief. Instead of turning off the water, she was mopping up the water, just mopping it up with all her energy. The water kept running out of the pail onto the floor, overflowing. They later sent her to Central Iceslip, that's a crazy house as they were known then, up in Long Island.

Adam got a letter from her about a week later. She told him to come and get her, that she was ready to come home. She wrote that there had been a dance and she didn't have anyone to dance with. She finally died in that institution, poor thing. I don't know if she ever really understood what was going on, but I prayed to God that there weren't any more like her in the congregation.

CHAPTER 11

Eleanor Blue

No father was ever prouder of a son than when Adam decided to go into the ministry. Adam had intended to go to medical school but changed his mind when he felt the calling and since some of his grades weren't so strong. The church had been grooming Adam for the position since birth. He would start as an assistant pastor and then take over fully for his father. The only problem was me. Old Man Powell and the church thought our "infatuation" was nothing more than a passing fancy. They couldn't have been more wrong.

When Adam graduated from Colgate University in upstate New York in 1930, his father sent him on a trip halfway around the world. Adam was supposed to forget me. He told his father that he wouldn't even contact me, but absence makes the heart grow fonder. Adam cabled and wrote to me constantly. He told me all about Egypt and the Holy Land, and brought me the most exquisite vials of perfume. Adam always had a mind of his own, and when he came home several months later, it was still fixed on me.

The Depression was still choking Harlem. But in 1930, three years before we married, the Harlem that Adam came back to after his overseas trip was not the same place he had left. The job boom following World War I had ended. The Depression hit Harlem hard, leaving ugly conditions on the streets. Many in our community had lost their jobs, were being evicted, and didn't have enough to eat; I mean they were really starving. We saw children with extended bellies, people shivering without coats, and others willing to work for pennies an hour. Neither Adam nor I had ever seen the kind of poverty that swallowed up Harlem during the Depression. He knew the church had to help. We started thinking about different projects and how to implement them. In the meantime, I had to make a formal transition into the church to show them I was part of the family now.

When Old Man Powell couldn't get rid of me any other way, he tried to drown me. He never would admit to it, but he did. He insisted I at least be baptized because I was going to marry his son. Adam thought it was a good idea. It would look right to the church. I went along, but it would take more than water to wash away all of my sins. After all, I was going to be the First Lady of Abyssinia. It sounded like a royal title to me. Adam explained exactly what was going to happen, but I was still nervous.

It was Sunday morning. I went around to the back side of the pulpit and stepped into a long white shroud. The sleeves were a little long and it fastened at the back. I felt trapped. Old Man Powell met me in the pool after walking down the steps at the opening behind the marble pulpit. His face was clean-shaven and pale. He wore a gown and looked like a ghost. The temperature of the water was lukewarm. He was so much bigger than me, almost like a giant. My heart was beating fast. I wanted to get it over with.

He said a few words about the Father, Son, and the Holy Ghost. Then he pressed his open palm down hard on my face, covering my mouth. I took a deep breath before I fell back into the water and closed my eyes. The next thing I knew, I was struggling to get air, but Old Man Powell held my head under the water. He must have known that I couldn't breathe because I shook my head and tried to remove his hand from my mouth and swung my arms. Nothing seemed to work. I knew this would be the end of me. I bulged my eyes open and tried to breathe again. After what seemed like a very long time, at the very last moment, he finally let go.

I came up gasping for air, my chest heaving. Once I had steadied myself and stood up, Old Man Powell just looked down at me with a calm straight face. I turned to look out at the congregation and was stared at by a line of pretty faces from the Cotton Club. They were dressed to the nines and their presence made me smile. The church's eyes were glued to them. I knew my girls couldn't believe that I had actually gone through with it, been baptized. Once I saw them staring, I tried to straighten up quickly like it was nothing. After all the stunts we had pulled on and off stage, I didn't want them to think that I was afraid of a mere baptism. Church was a lot more tame than the night life in Harlem, or so I thought.

When I told Adam about Father Powell's attempt to murder me, he said I was overreacting. His father was just a little heavy-handed. He would have done it the very same way. Maybe.

"Bunny, come on now. He didn't mean anything. None of that will matter once we get married. You'll be his daughter-in-law, and he'll accept you. I'll make sure of that. I promise. I would never let anybody hurt you. You know that." He pulled me to him and covered my entire body with his. Then he started talking about how much planning we still needed to do for the wedding. He had just said the magic word, I couldn't be mad anymore. I managed to push the episode to the back of my mind but I knew I had better stay on guard.

One thing I didn't have to worry about was the relationship between Adam and my son, Preston. Preston adored Adam and Adam took Preston in like his own. I saw that Adam would be both a wonderful father and husband.

Franklin Roosevelt was one of the most popular presidents to have ever run this country. Most of the colored folk in Harlem were for Roosevelt so we watched the election closely. When he was sworn in the first time, on March 4th, 1933, all eyes were on his wife. He didn't seem to mind sharing the limelight either. I'll never forget it. The color of her dress was absolutely stunning, but it was her quiet presence and soft dignity that made the dress. Turning heads like no other First Lady had done before earned her her own color. When you walked into a shop and asked for Eleanor Blue, people knew exactly what you meant. It would be the perfect color for my wedding dress.

Except for the rainstorm pouring down over the city, my wedding day, Wednesday, March 8th, 1933, was absolutely perfect. Fredi and I took a taxi from 136th Street. The church was only a few blocks away. It was still early in the morning, but people were beginning to line up and congregate outside the church. Some people actually paid for window space in the buildings across the street so they could hang out the windows and catch a glimpse of us. Inside, there was so much hustle and bustle, it felt like the holidays. Old Man Powell was the first person I ran into. He greeted me in the aisle at the front of the church just below the pulpit with a polite nod and a quick smile. So many times he had called me Jezebel and not even under his breath. How would it feel to have Jezebel as a daughter-in-law and the mother of your only grandchildren? It served him right for calling me that.

Fredi and I went upstairs to get dressed and for hair and make-up. Both of our dresses were custom designed just for the wedding. My dress was delicate Eleanor Blue, trimmed in appliquéd lace with a half-back yolk. Lace covered my back and arms down to my wrists. It was just gorgeous. I wore a matching blue ringlet hat and heeled slippers. I knew it was raining cats and dogs outside, but once I put on my gown, I was blinded by the light and couldn't see anything but sunshine. Fredi was my maid of honor. She wore a lovely soft peach long sleeved satin dress, also trimmed in lace. It's a wonder she made the wedding at all. She was in a play that had just opened in March at the Lyric Theater, *Run, Little Chillin*. All the planning, the fittings, the invitations, everything, all came down to this day. I was so nervous and excited. Everything had to be perfect.

Once we put on my make-up, I had to force myself not to cry. That's just how happy I was. Shortly after noon, Fredi and I entered the main sanctuary from the left. When I heard the guests suck in their breath, I knew I must have looked absolutely exquisite. Adam took my breath away, tall and handsome in his formal black tux with a corsage just above the breast pocket. I held onto the bridal bouquet of orchid lilies like it was my last friend in the world. I didn't want to drop it and be embarrassed in front of all of these people. The church was absolutely packed. I was just so nervous. I couldn't believe I was doing this again, getting married. But this time I wasn't a silly teenager. We had dated for about three years and he was a man of the cloth, the one I would be with for the rest of my life.

A number of my show-business friends came to the wedding. Several rows in the balcony were filled with petite beauties from both Connie's Inn and the Cotton Club, including my close friend Maude Russell. Each one was fabulously dressed. They knew they couldn't come to my wedding looking any other kind of way. The church couldn't help but gawk.

I had been inside these tall imposing walls so many times – Italian marble and all the righteous things this place stood for - the sermons, the prayers, the baptism. Mother Powell and other parishioners had shown me such kindness. Now I was walking down the aisle about to marry my Prince Charming. To think, initially, I didn't even want to go to church with him. Lots of great memories were locked inside these walls. I took a breath and moved forward. I knew I would always be safe and welcomed here.

The ceremony was brief. We left out the word "obey." But as I stood next to Adam saying, "I do," I knew that I was marrying one of the greatest men in the world.

The reception was downstairs in the community house of the church where the kitchen is. There were literally hundreds of gifts in the basement nearby. It looked like a store with something for everyone - large and small boxes with the most beautiful wrappings. I was overwhelmed. There were rolling pins, silver candlesticks, crystal bowls, platters trimmed in gold, so many things, many of which I still have and use.

I was so touched that I made sure to respond in writing to each person who had sent a gift. Once we returned from our honeymoon, I wrote until it felt like my fingers were no longer attached to my hand. Then, I'd take a break and get right back to it until each gift had been acknowledged with a proper thank you. I had to start off right as Mrs. Adam Clayton Powell Jr. The last thing I needed was some mother of the church saying I didn't acknowledge her wedding gift.

The crowds at the church and in the street were just incredible. I shook at least two thousand hands and gave out about two thousand miniature boxes of wedding cake. Big Momma, bless her heart, had made a huge cake. She would not have her Belle eating anybody else's cake on her wedding day. It was delicious. Everyone kept telling us what a lovely couple we were and how beautiful we looked together. It was a truly amazing day. I was so flattered that I thought it was never going to end. By the time we finished I was absolutely exhausted. Even though I was certain my arm would fall off if I had to shake one more hand, my face was fixed into a permanent smile. I didn't want anyone to think I was ungrateful.

We spent the first part of our honeymoon in farming country in Lynchburgh, Va. It was so green and quiet. The morning after our arrival, I went out in search of the madam of the house. She was in the yard behind the house with her back to me, sitting on a little stool holding a bowl under a cow's udders. I greeted her and asked what she was doing.

"Getting milk for the cake," she said. I had never seen anything like it before. I had to laugh and I must admit that that was one of the best cakes I have ever tasted.

Adam insisted on spending a few days up at Martha's Vineyard too. He had been coming to the island with his family since he was a young boy. It was second nature to him. He seemed to know everyone. And each time he introduced me as his wife, my heart jumped and I knew I would be happy forever. It was a bit too cold to get into the water but Adam talked about how we would fish and swim and just have a great time when we came back in the summer.

He took me to Shearer Cottage at Oak Bluffs. Shearer is one of the island's treasures that various black professionals, artists, and politicians have patronized for years, and kept as their little secret. The flowers, shrubs, grass and rocks gave the place a homey cozy feel that I loved. The fact that it's owned and run by blacks made me take even more pride in our visit to Shearer. Off from the main house, to one side, there was a row of barrack type rooms. Adam and I stayed in one of these studios.

Our room was simple and elegant, about 12 square feet, with a chamber pot underneath the large bed. A bureau, nightstand, and colorful landscapes on the wall completed the room. Chaise lounges and wicker furniture decorated the various porches around the house. The dining area which fed twelve rooms was large. The food was so delicious that even people who were just visiting the island came by regularly for meals if there was room. None of us could get enough of the hominy grits, fish cakes, and sweet potatoes, or the homemade desserts of peach ice cream, cobbler, and lemon cake. The service was top notch.

It was our habit to dress for dinner. We wanted to look our best. It wasn't just the shiny new Buicks and winged Thunderbirds that got us from one place to the next. We were New Yorkers, who had to set the style, to be that example for the next one who would follow in our footsteps. Except for the mosquitoes and earwigs, I was living a fantasy.

On the lawn outside the room, Adam and I played kickball. One of the other guests, a Mr. Bolton, who wrote deep Negro spirituals, complained that we made too much noise. After a few complaints to Sadie, the owner, Adam finally told him that it was too bad if he thought we were making too much noise. If the noise disturbed him that much, why didn't he get a place way out in the woods where no one would bother him and he could write his music. We didn't hear too many complaints after that.

We returned from our honeymoon and I began my real life as Mrs. Adam Clayton Powell Jr. I couldn't think, say, or hear that name enough. I busied myself with learning people's names and a number of church activities. I never thought I could be this happy. My first marriage had been nothing like this. I didn't care to think much about my first marriage or Preston Webster. He was part of my past and my future looked so bright. I didn't really want to thing about the Depression either, but it stared us in the face everyday when we went outside. The Depression had done a number on Harlem, but it never even passed by me and Adam. Old Man Powell had plenty of money and the church would see to it that its assistant pastor was comfortable so he could focus his attention on the needs of the people.

We lived over the church in those days in several rooms

at the parsonage. We settled into a comfortable daily routine. We always looked forward to Wednesdays, his day off. Generally we spent the day together relaxing and enjoying each other. But one morning Adam went out and not long after came running in as white as a sheet. He sat down in a chair breathing so hard with his hand on his chest. I asked him what was wrong. "You'll never believe this story," he said.

There was a woman in the church who had been hounding him, I mean really hounding him. She got on the phone and had someone call Adam to say she was deathly ill. She lived right around the corner from the church and asked if he would please come. He thought the woman might be dying. He went to the address and rang the doorbell. When she opened the door, she was stark naked! She grabbed him and pulled him inside. He tried to compose himself and backed up against the door. He really didn't know what to do. It was one of those houses that has the French doors in between the living room and the bedroom. It was open and the bed was all laid back and everything, you know, prepared for a rendezvous.

He told her that she really shouldn't do this, that he had understood she was sick. He told her he had a very important engagement and needed to leave immediately. She said she was sick for him and had been wanting him a long time. She couldn't move him towards her bed. He had never moved from the entryway. He fumbled with the door with his hands behind him until he got it open. Then he ran. He flew out of there. He was really in shock. He came home to me, his wife. He never went on a sick visit after that. He would have his assistants go.

I kept the story at the back of my mind. Even though I was the pastor's wife, I saw how other women looked at Adam. Sometimes I could feel and smell how they lusted after him. When Adam would call for all the sinners to come forth on Sundays, he would drop his head forward and open his arms wide in a paternal gesture. When some of the same women came up to the alter several times, it was clear that seeking God's forgiveness was the last thing on their mind. They wanted to get close to Adam anyway they could. But my Bunny Boy was fully devoted to me. I knew I had nothing to worry about.

The first three months of my marriage to Adam passed so very quickly. I tried to be the perfect wife, paying attention to every last detail. Adam made it easy. Wingie, the one-armed chauffeur, drove me everywhere I needed to go. A cook assisted me with wonderful dinners. The table seated twenty-four and we had guests frequently. I invited Elyse and her family often. A maid helped me to keep the place tidy. I never had to buy so much as a pair of stockings. My Bunny took care of everything. I knew my house was in order. I told Maude that I was set for life. I related the incident about the woman from church and concluded that Adam was an extraordinary man, unlike most. I didn't have to worry about him. Maude was happy for me but wasn't so sure about me being set for life. "He *is* a man," she reminded me. And then she added, "Like father, like son." I just shook my head and we laughed it off. She couldn't possibly realize how special Adam was.

I tried to include at least a few new people on our dinner guest list each time we had people over to the parsonage. I was convinced that if more members got to know me even a little, they would like me ad accept me fully into the church. After one particular engagement, the maid told me that one of the forks was missing. She couldn't find it anywhere. A few days later, I received a very nice letter from one of the women who had attended. She had enjoyed the dinner and conversation so much that she kept the fork to remember the occasion. I hoped that she had a great memory because she would never be invited back again. The never of her, she thought it okay to take the fork as long as she confessed her act of thievery which was in such bad taste.

Even though my husband was only the assistant pastor, his transition to pastor had already begun. Some events I had to attend as the wife of the pastor and others I went to because it was the right thing to do. I busied myself with a number of activities until after a while I no longer even thought about the Cotton Club or Broadway. I didn't need either because I had Adam, or rather we had each other. Going to bed before midnight took a little getting used to, but after a while I managed just fine. Essentially I found ways to transfer the theater into the church. Adam had brought Abyssinia to the Cotton Club and I had completed the journey by bringing the club back into the church. I organized plays, fashion shows, and all kinds of events especially for the youth of the church.

The choirs I directed took me back to my days in Savannah. I wanted to give these children a reason to look forward to coming to church, not scare them away. There were several choirs ranging across various age groups, a hundred young voices. When we rehearsed and performed for the church, you couldn't have told me that I wasn't directing angels straight from heaven. One little angel in particular has grown up and done quite well for herself, Diahnne Carroll, a model of grace and decorum. I am so proud of her. Occasionally we run into each other and she always speaks.

June arrived sooner than I could imagine. We made arrangements to go back to the island. It would be my first summer there. The water was warm, the fish was fresh, and the people were simply delightful. Not even as an actress on Broadway had I been invited out to so many lunches. Adam came up as much as he could, mostly on the weekends.

One weekend, when Adam had come up to the island, he decided that it was time for me to learn how to swim. We were in the sound, in the area just off the beach. I wore my swimsuit, my swim cap, and just a touch of make-up. Adam was standing in the water showing me how to scoop the water in a sweeping motion. I was getting the hang of it, when he squatted lower into the water so I could really practice. I'm not that well endowed and wore falsies at the time, little cotton puffs to amplify the bosom. Well, one of them decided it wanted to swim out on its own. I hadn't even realized that it was gone. Adam extended a closed fist to me. He was holding back a laugh until he placed it in my hand.

"I believe this belongs to you," he said with a devious smile.

I began to cry. I have never ever been so embarrassed in my entire life. I grabbed the puff and replaced it where it belonged.

"I don't want to learn to swim," I continued to cry. "I'm getting out of this water right now."

"Bunny, Bunny, Bunny!" he tried to call me back but he couldn't stop laughing. Of course, that only made me madder. Eventually, I got over my embarrassment. Adam assured me that he adored me and loved me just the way I was. I have long ago given up the falsies, but the sheer embarrassment of that incident comes back to mind each time I consider learning how to swim, so I don't.

Marriage had become the most wonderful word in the English language. When my big sister got married for the first time later that year, I couldn't have been happier. I also couldn't believe that I had done something, experienced such a wonderful thing, before Sister. Little sisters are supposed to follow not precede big sisters. Fredi married Lawrence Brown, a top trombone player from Duke Ellington's band. She and the Duke used to be sweethearts at one time but they got mad about something and Fredi took off. Fredi left for overseas in a huff and when she got back, the Duke had hooked up with one of her girlfriends. So much for best girlfriends.

Lawrence joined the band in about 1932 and he was so quiet that the band members and chorus girls kind of thought there was something wrong with him. He was shy and really stood out from the other band members. He didn't really talk to anyone. Fredi made a bet with the other dancers that she could make him talk. She won the bet. That wager led to marriage. Fredi and Lawrence were happy, but both of them had demanding careers. The Duke Ellington band was always in demand, and her acting and dancing kept her quite busy, so that sometimes she and Lawrence were in different cities and on opposite sides of the country. When he was away on tour with the Duke she wrote him a letter every day. He called her Fritz. Way back then, trains and not planes were the primary mode of travel and only fairly wealthy people actually had their own cars. Crossing the country took several days, by car or train.

Adam and I hadn't been married that long when a producer approached us about playing Romeo and Juliet in a play. It was tempting for me and flattering for Adam, but the church didn't want him to have anything to do with the stage. We said no.

The country was still struggling to recover from the financial disasters of the Crash of Wall Street. Banks failed all around and there was massive unemployment. Roosevelt gave us some hope with his New Deal Programs including social security, but giving people back their liquor really made him even more popular. By the end of 1933, Roosevelt got rid of Prohibition and made liquor a state matter. Maybe the government realized the tax on booze was helping the gangsters and mobsters more than it was helping the government to climb out of the Depression. Whatever the reason, Harlem seemed to smile now that people could drink in the open. Adam continued to do what he had always done: hold a drink in one hand, a cigar in the other, and with me by his side, he celebrated his wonderful life.

CHAPTER 12

Queen of Harlem

Now that I was Mrs. Adam Clayton Powell Jr., I could show everyone that preachers and showgirls *did* belong in the same family. They're cut from the same cloth. I would simply be a different kind of showgirl, a showgirl for God so to speak. My background in the theater prepared me for practically anything. I could face any situation and surely I could manage a few indignant members of the congregation. This was a church after all.

One of the reasons Adam and I got along so well is that we both knew how to have a good time. On any given occasion, Adam was rarely without a smile, a drink, and his cigar. He enjoyed the spotlight as much as me, probably more. If you can't tolerate the spotlight, you can't be with someone who's in the spotlight because occasionally it will focus on you. When it fell on me, I'd give them my brightest Broadway smile, and look over at my adoring husband, confident in the warmth and fidelity of our relationship.

Not only did Adam love to have a good time, he loved to do it with lots of people around. He was sort of a real life Pied Piper because he attracted people so easily like honey bees. From time to time, when we got back to the apartment at night, I would just breathe and listen to the still air because it was so quiet. As Adam became more involved in politics, those moments became fewer and fewer.

My husband was generous to a fault. When people were in need, he'd give them money right out of his pocket. It hurt him to see anyone in pain. When we were still courting, he brought me flowers or perfume "just because." Or he might pick up a special gift because he was thinking about me. After we married, he didn't change. He was absolutely the most thoughtful man alive. I loved it. I loved him. There was nothing I wouldn't have done for him. When we first met we really weren't that serious. We were just keeping company with each other and having the time of our lives. He was tall, handsome, well educated, and all the girls wanted him. And I, of course, could match him. I was a beautiful Cotton Club dancer, with a Broadway acting and singing career staring me in the face. Any number of suitors were trying to date me. I took extra care getting dressed for each date, sometimes piling my dark auburn hair in curls atop my head and other times letting it fall down to my shoulders.

I never imagined myself with anyone who had anything to do with the church, but God does work in mysterious ways. As we began to fall in love with each other, as I have mentioned, the Old Man did his best to break us apart. I think his determination to keep us away from each other was in part what brought us together. It wasn't enough just to date or even marry, we had to *prove* him wrong by staying married, remaining devoted to each other, and having a family so we could celebrate a diamond anniversary.

It was hard for me to believe that someone with Father Powell's past was so concerned about me. Before Old Man Powell donned a preacher's robe, he was known to imbibe rather heavily and admitted that he had been somewhat of a lowlife and a lady's man. But like his son, he was tall, fair-skinned, full of presence, and knew that he was destined for more. He left New Haven and came to New York City to pastor a reasonably sized church in Lower Manhattan. The church had been founded by Ethiopians who tired of racial mistreatment at the white church where they worshipped. The new church grew quickly and moved to larger premises. Old Man Powell won over resistant parishioners and in 1923 oversaw the move of this Negro church to mostly white Harlem where it remains today. Given his own "colorful" past, I didn't see why he objected to my past. He turned out okay and so would I.

I didn't think we'd ever win over the "old curmudgeon," as Adam sometimes called his father. But eventually Old Man Powell stopped calling me Jezebel and at least tolerated me in a respectful way. Despite all his efforts, Adam and I were now married and we had a fabulous life together. On Sunday mornings, Adam would get up around 7:00 in the morning to go downstairs and write his sermon. I'd stay in bed. When he had finished, he'd bring me my coffee in bed. It was always in a little silver coffee pot on a little silver tray.

Adam would deliver a fiery sermon in church to which

the people would nod their heads in agreement or say, "Amen." Occasionally there would be a little too much feedback from the pews. This one woman who just loved Adam would shout during almost any point of the church service. She'd come right out and say, "Hallelujah! Thank you Jesus! Praise God!" loudly. Then she'd raise her hands to God and repeat it again a bit louder to be certain Adam had heard her. One morning she caught Adam in a bad mood. The very first time she did it, Adam turned directly to her and said, "Sister Hallelujah, there ain't gonna be but one preacher in this house and that's me." I know he hated to embarrass her like that, but he was able to get through the sermon without interruption that day. The congregation was grateful.

If Adam had worn a light linen suit the week before, we'd see lots of the men in white linen suits. He liked to look good and I didn't mind. They loved to dress like him. If he saw someone in an outfit similar to one he had, he'd go up to them and tell them how sharp they looked that day. Adam's quick handshake and warm smile made everyone feel good.

After church, Adam was also fond of wearing his tails and striped pants. We used to walk down Seventh Avenue. I'd be wearing one of my best outfits, walking right beside him down 125th Street where the building is now named for him. We would be greeting people and smiling the whole time. Parishioners and people in the community would tell us what a lovely couple we made and that they were so glad to have us in the community. Then we'd walk back to the church. If men were standing in a store front, he'd break away from me, walk over to them, grab both of their hands in his and say, "Hi, my friend." He would even greet bums on the street, it didn't matter. If they wanted to share a concern with him, he would listen, everyone counted to him.

Sometimes we would have dinner at the church because they served dinner practically every Sunday downstairs in the community room. Frequently they served chicken, you know black folks always have to have chicken! All the sisters in the kitchen could cook too. They'd have it looking like Thanksgiving in there. There would be greens, my favorite, potato salad, baked macaroni and cheese, string beans, and every other kind of dish they thought Adam might like.

Occasionally we'd go downtown to dinner at one of our favorite restaurants. Our absolute favorite place was the Oyster House over on 42nd Street. This place is one of the oldest and most fabulous eating establishments in New York City. We were both very fond of seafood: crabs, lobsters, snails, and oysters. Just like I could eat anywhere I wanted no matter the price, I felt that I could have anything I wanted. When we compared our lives to the typical Harlemite, Adam and I both felt terrible. Here we were, married, living in a nice warm place over the church, taking up several rooms, with all the food in the world, but so many people in the street didn't have bread or shelter. We had to find a way to resolve this dilemma.

Adam decided the church would open a soup kitchen and help feed the starving people of Harlem. His idea was great. I got busy right away organizing things. The sisters of the church came in early in the morning and started preparing food. I was right there helping to prepare dishes, serving food and taking care of people. It was the saddest thing I had ever seen. Blocks and blocks of people standing in line for a bowl of hot soup. For some this might be their only meal of the week.

Adam was coming into his own and wanted to help people any way he could. It wasn't only the poor people who lost their jobs, several doctors over at Harlem Hospital were also let go because they were Negro. Adam organized the Committee on Harlem Hospital too, and by the time he was finished with his mass meetings and pickets, the doctors had their jobs back, the staff at the hospital was integrated, and the place was sanitized. Part of the problem with the hospital had been that the community it served was primarily black so no one cared. But Adam cared and he made others care. People who had no interest in politics took an interest when they found out they had a voice. When Adam was younger, Old Man Powell told him to always stay in the public eye, no matter what. Adam took that piece of advice to heart. Now he knew how to remain in the public eye. He was in his twenties, on an unbelievable high, and he knew he was on to something. It was a tremendous victory for all of us.

At first my help was limited. I went to the marches, pickets, and protests so that I could be seen and heard. I called on friends from the Cotton Club, Connie's Inn and various theater companies. Any way we could increase the numbers, we did. I made phone calls, helped with trainings, and ran off mimeographs of sheets we needed to post and hand out. I was still working at the club. But once we got married and I quit working, I threw myself into the church, just like I was starring in my dream role on Broadway or in Hollywood. I was right there with Adam working in the soup kitchen so people could have at least one hot meal every couple of days.

Both Fredi and I used our connections in the entertainment world to get people to perform at Abyssinia. They gave all kinds of shows, from singing and dancing to speeches. We knew we had done something special when Ethel Waters, not your nicest person, agreed to perform. That alone was a significant victory. But when Marcus Garvey gave talks, people came in droves. Most people had no intention of following him back to Africa, but they came out to hear what he had to say. We were grateful. At these affairs, I typically raised anywhere from $4,000 to $25,000.

Fredi was one of the founders as well as an officer of the Negro Actor's Guild. Her call brought out tons of people to the various marches and demonstrations. Adam knew people in the entertainment arena, too, because he frequented the clubs and shows so much, but now that the two of us had a united front the numbers swelled to sizes we had never imagined. Each and every person had come out to support the cause.

Adam realized that Abyssinia *was* his core, the belly of the fight for civil rights. If the church mentioned a march or protest from the pulpit, then it was sure to be overflowing. We worked tirelessly to bring more people into the church and to increase its visibility in the community. Membership at Abyssinia increased by the thousands making it much easier for us to get noticed. We made demands on local businesses that would have repercussions across the state of New York. They gave in as our numbers increased. Adam just ate it all up. He loved the intimate connection between Abyssinia and the demand for civil rights. He knew his church, like me, would do anything to please him. It was a win-win situation.

In the community, when people saw my face, they thought of Abyssinia and came to church. We put on fashion shows and organized plays to raise funds for the church. My heart went out to the young people. I wanted them to have better opportunities than I did. We worked with them on their speech and made sure they knew how to talk to people when the opportunities arose. In one of the plays, my son Preston Jr., played Popeye the Sailorman. He curled up his bicep to show how strong he was and held up a can of spinach. It was so very cute.

I could see that this was Adam's calling. He was on top of the world when he was helping people. And I was right by his side doing whatever I could to help, supporting him in every way. Funny, sometimes when I came back from a protest and could barely get my shoes off, or I was on a tight schedule doing a show for the kids, I felt very much like I was back on Broadway. Just like Adam was doing what he was born to do, so was I and I knew it. We protested the lack of blacks at the utility companies. We made the telephone company give up racist policies, made it possible for blacks to lease stores on 125th Street where we spent probably millions of dollars, and would not rest until the Fifth Avenue Bus Company hired black drivers.

The church and now Harlem at large loved its Adam.

All of my life I had wanted to be a star, to be on stage or screen, to be recognized by name or face, to give brilliant performances where I had given my all and made people happy. It occurred to me that I was indeed a star. I had more than anyone could want and was recognized almost anywhere I went. People referred to me as the Queen of Harlem, a most appropriate title since I was married to the King of Harlem. I was determined to work hard to remain worthy of the title.

Despite everything that was going on, Adam and I still found the time and energy to go out and have a little fun. It was this side of Adam that some of the elder members of the church objected to. And for those who could, it seemed like the worse things got economically, the more people needed their entertainment, to let their hair down.

Sometimes we had these Sunday night soirees at home. Everyone who was anyone in Harlem came. Various topics of discussion would come up, or we'd just be listening to music, but we always had a great time. I remember a particular evening when I had made Creole tripe which Old Man Powell liked. Walter White, an executive for the NAACP, was there and Judge Delaney, the younger brother of the Delaney sisters, was getting ready to leave. I brought Judge Delaney in the kitchen because he hadn't had anything to eat yet. He said he'd seen enough of that tripe in the South and he didn't want any. So I opened up another pot and offered him some rice. He said, "Who cooked that rice?" I told him I had. So he said to give him a little gravy on the rice and he would taste it. When he tasted it, he asked for some tripe. And from that day until he died, his wife had to make Creole tripe for him. That's just how good a cook I had become, thanks to Mother Powell.

Even though I had a cook, I prepared a lot of the meals myself. Because Mrs. Powell had treated me like her own daughter and had taught me many of her cooking secrets, I was dangerous in the kitchen and I loved to show off. If someone requested something special for the next party, I'd make a note of it, have the cook go shopping, and prepare a small feast for our friends. Had it not been for Mother Powell, Adam, like my first husband, would have starved to death. I couldn't boil water when we got married. I still have most of her pots and pans.

We had a wonderful relationship. She was German, a lovely woman. I used to go to prayer meeting and sit with her. There was a little black woman who used to come too. I remember the woman because her mouth was full of gold. She'd come and sit right down beside us and then she'd testify. She'd get up and start, "Ah, Jesus, Oh, Jesus is hanging on the cross and He had nothing but a diaper to hide his shame." Every Friday night she would repeat the same thing. And Mother Powell and I would look at each other like here we go again. The church didn't really pay her no mind. They just let her jump up and have her good time.

Week after week, success after success rolled in. Important people in politics would contact Adam and sometimes people gave large sums of money to help support the cause. It was almost as if Adam could do no wrong. He really hadn't thought about going into politics. His father had been getting sick and planned on stepping down so Adam could take over. Old Man Powell and I didn't agree on much, but we both thought that running for City Council was something Adam should NOT do. It would leave a lot less time for the church and would place Adam in uncharted territory. No black had ever served on the City Council before.

Once Adam got the idea in his head, there was absolutely no changing his mind. Both his father and I stepped on board and supported him. I let him know that I loved him dearly and would support any action he took even if I didn't agree with it.

He felt that running was the best thing to do because politics in Harlem, a black enclave, was controlled by whites who didn't care at all about the community. He thought the best way to really make some changes was to do it from above. While I agreed with him in part, I knew that politics was different from religion. It was about 1941 when Adam announced that he would be running. No one was surprised. Adam and I had been married for eight years. I knew him well enough to know that his ego could handle religion but I wasn't so certain if it could handle politics.

He had little money for his campaign initially but he had a lot of bodies to do work. The way the electoral system was set up, no black could be elected for Harlem without support from the other areas. This election was really an impossible feat, but Adam had achieved the impossible before.

There were ninety-nine candidates. Adam campaigned himself ragged, up and down the street, in the church, practically everywhere. He ran as an Independent so he wouldn't be beholden to either party. When he saw the ballot, he thought it might be confusing to the voters so he mailed out over 200,000 sample ballots to show the voters exactly how to vote. As a result, Harlem had the least number of spoiled ballots and Adam got about 50,000 first place votes. When it was all said and done, Adam had received the third highest vote overall, and New York City had elected its first Negro councilman. Once again Adam had achieved the impossible.

I did not agree with his running, and I still had my reservations, but I was right there on January 1st, 1942, when Mayor La Guardia swore him in. I had to support my husband.

I wondered how Adam would manage to balance his competing duties. I prayed that integrity, a quality that appeared to be rare in New York politics, would be high up on the list. I still saw him as a preacher, a pastor, and a loving, devoted husband, a role model for all of Abyssinia. But this political thing was much larger, maybe even a bit scary. God, I hoped he wouldn't change.

Adam was an awesome preacher who liked to use everyday things as the topics of his messages. One time he talked about, "What's in your hand?" When he said you couldn't keep your hand in a fist because you would be unable to give or receive anything, people were already beginning to shout, "Hallelujahs" and "Amens." These people loved him so. They should not be short-changed if politics became more important to him.

I saw him walking up and down the pulpit, using his hands and his body to make a point, always standing tall and erect. He charmed people by making each and everyone feel that they were important, like he was preaching directly to them. He knew most of the church by name, and knew what was going on in their lives. He'd congratulate this one on a child's graduation and that one on some other important event. It really was amazing to watch. I just didn't know if he could do the same thing in the political arena. Part of me thought he had it so good here that he didn't need to venture outside. Another part of me was afraid. It had taken so long and was so difficult for me to be accepted by this church, by these people, I didn't want to go through anything like that ever again. It had reminded me of the pledging process students go through in college. I had crossed over and didn't want to ever pledge again.

I did all kinds of things to blend in and be accepted by the church. I had a club at the church called the Junior League. It raised money to take care of old folks' homes. The girls would come to meetings and they would smoke cigarettes. I did it too, just like a child following along because I saw them do it. I would puff away at my one cigarette and think I was big, cool, one of the girls.

To show my Bunny Boy how much I was with him in this political game, I used to attend some of the meetings at the council. I paid close attention at the meetings. I wanted to understand what was going on and be able to discuss any questions he might have for me. But more than anything, I wanted to show him that I supported him.

Adam's eyes would light up when he talked about the various programs and projects that the city should do for the people.

Everyone could see that he really cared. He was able to put Harlem on the map in New York City, but however much he got done, it was never enough. The need was so great. When I thought he was exhausted from his work at the council, he would come back to the parsonage, light up a cigar, have a drink and head to the church to do it all over again.

Instead of the tug between the church and politics I had been concerned about, Adam made the church the backbone of his politics. When he wanted to propose something new to the council, he would preach it to Abyssinia first. They loved their councilman so, that they would gobble up almost anything he said. He just knew that they would go along with him even before he presented his ideas, because what was good for Adam, was good for Abyssinia, and Harlem, and everybody else. For a long time it worked out just fine and no one questioned his motives. Adam and I were the talk of the town and not just in the black parts of the city. It was truly amazing.

CHAPTER 13

Colored and Proud

Adam was always for the underdog. In 1941 when he won the election for City Council, Harlem was the underdog. People were stacked on top of each other, squeezing into any nook and cranny they could find. While this made the city exciting, because you could literally run into anyone, there was no denying that the place was overcrowded. More people arrived on a daily basis it seemed. The people were so poor and many didn't have jobs. It was almost a hopeless situation. On top of that, the country was at war. Colored men were sent to war and made to fight for a freedom they themselves didn't have.

The conditions in Harlem were very much like the play *Harlem* that I had been starring in when I met Adam. It began and ended with a rent party because no one could afford to pay the rent. The partygoers bought pigs feet and drinks prepared by the hosts. That's how they earned enough money to pay the rent. There was lots of shucking and jiving, and showing out because people had so little. In the play I ran off with a numbers runner. There were nearly one hundred people in the cast. That's a lot of bodies on one stage, a lot of sweat, and a lot of attitudes.

With his new title, Councilman, all kinds of people, black, white, and everything in between, called on Adam for help. He tried to help them all. It's one of the reasons he became so popular. He proposed legislation that would make everyone's life better and put the city on notice that the underdog now had a voice and a loud one at that. He fought for decent housing conditions and argued that America was asking the Negro to fight overseas for rights he didn't have here at home.

Adam liked to make people face their fears about race. He especially liked making racist whites feel uncomfortable about their misconceptions concerning other people. Once, we were on a train taking a trip in the South. We had been heading for the dining car when Adam fell into a conversation with this white man who began to talk about, "niggers." As he pointed out the window, the man made derogatory comments about the people picking cotton in the fields. After just a few moments, Adam turned to the man and said, "Well, you're talking to niggers!" Just to let him know that we weren't afraid of him, Adam waited a few seconds to see if the guy would respond. His face turned a purplish red. The man was so embarrassed and flustered he didn't know what to do. We turned and headed for the dining car. Adam loved scenes like that.

Another time Adam was giving a speech and as he stood up to move toward the podium, he said something like he came not as an elected official but as a Negro. Everyone was flustered and you could hear people begin to whisper because he didn't look like your average colored person. They were asking who he was and what he was.

I stood by him as he demanded fairness and civil rights for Harlemites and anyone else who was being oppressed. As he stood up and fought, Adam saw that the City Council had little power to effectively change the lives of constituents. He set his eyes higher. He had had a taste of power and after that there was no way to quench his thirst.

At a powerful rally held at Madison Square Garden in 1942, full of wall to wall Negroes, the man of the hour didn't even get to speak because Adam just took over the crowd. He was reminding folks of some of the recent victories we had achieved with the marching, pickets, protests, and what not and said that he needed to run for Congress to represent this new Negro. The place erupted. That was Adam. He hadn't long been sworn onto the City Council and was already heading toward Congress. He couldn't see what was happening to him, but I could and I was not happy. I asked him not to run. He practically ignored me.

In order to get his message out all over town, Adam started a paper called *The People's Voice*. I took great interest in this paper not only because it was Adam's paper, but also because he had appointed Fredi as Theater Editor and Columnist. She wrote about a variety of topics and the column was well received. Her picture appeared in the paper every week. She made snazzy comments about the issue of the moment. Adam and Fredi got along very well. He thought she was very talented and we went to see her perform from time to time. But I think what he liked most about Fredi is what we all had in common, being colored and proud.

Adam had to sort of grow into his pride. Perhaps it was because his mother, Mattie Powell, was German and he didn't want to deny that part of his heritage. Like my family in Savannah, for the most part, Adam was protected from the ugliness of racism by his economic status. But the young Negro boys in his new Harlem neighborhood saw only color and to them he looked white. They asked what he was. He took a moment to respond because no one had ever asked him that question. Then he looked down at his skin and told them he was white. He was beaten. The next night he encountered a gang of white boys who also wanted to know what he was. When he said colored, they beat him up too. The following night yet another group of Negro boys asked him what he was and he responded "mixed." They thought he said, "Mick," a common name for the Irish at the time and they beat him up. Adam learned that it was not how he looked on the exterior, but how he thought on the inside that made the difference and determined who he was.

When Adam was housed at Colgate, initially his room-mate was white. Once his "color" became known, his room-mate wanted him out and the few colored students who were on campus were not too pleased. They thought he had been trying to pass. Adam had not been trying to pass, but he did not make his ethnic background known. He could tell early on when he arrived that no one knew he was colored. He had even pledged to a white fraternity. But by the time he became a member of the New York City Council, he was the proudest colored man walking around. He knew who and what he was. And the beautiful thing about Adam was that just because he was colored, it didn't stop him from helping other groups, whether they were Indian, white, Hispanic, or even Communist. If someone kept Adam's goal in mind, he would work with them.

Now Fredi and I on the other hand had two colored parents who both happened to be light-skinned. My father actually looked kind of like a Jewish man. My mother was light too, Fredi looked just like her. From a very young age, Fredi and I had been taught that we were colored, and as we grew older, Fredi made sure I remembered this vital lesson. It was especially important for colored people as light as we were who were frequently mistaken for white.

Reporters called me a "sepia cabaret thrush," to show that I'm colored. Most people already knew that the Washington sisters were colored, colored and proud. Producers and such tried to get Fredi to go away for a while and then come back with some exotic or French name. They told her that her life would be much easier, she would be able to practice her craft, she would get more roles, and be much happier. She refused. "Passing," meant that it was better to be white, that colored people were inferior, and no one who was black could be happy. Neither of us could accept such foolishness. Fredi hated the idea that you had to be white to be good. Like Fredi, I'd been asked to change who I am, but I refused each time. I know who and what I am and I'm happy with that. Even though the terms have changed several times, I still consider myself a colored woman.

When people suggested that we could be "helpful" if we passed, even that we could not accept. We didn't create the system and are not responsible for our light complexions. Fredi said that she would fight racial prejudice forever, or stop when it didn't exist anymore. Of course, she knew it would be a very long time before racism would end in this country.

Race was always an issue when a show was on the road. Fredi adored Paul Robeson and was so nervous when she got the part opposite him in the play *Black Boy*. It was her first real role. She had been working as a principal dancer and was noticed by someone involved with the play. She was entirely unknown, but Paul let her use his dressing-room to help her relax a little. He was already famous and well known. He didn't have to be that nice, but he was. Fredi was grateful. When the play went on the road, Fredi had no problems when she checked into hotels. On the other hand, when Paul stepped up, all of a sudden no rooms were available. Fredi was ready to raise hell. She would fight anybody. Fortunately, a friend of Paul's came and got him so Paul could stay with him while he was in town.

This type of thing happened all the time when plays were on tour. It got so bad that if the hotel wouldn't let the others stay, Fredi would refuse to stay too. Once she was on the road with Duke Ellington. It was hot and they wanted some ice cream. Of course they couldn't go into the shop because they were in the South. So Fredi went into the shop and got them some ice cream. When she took it to her fellow performers, she was called a, "nigger lover."

Back at the clubs where we danced, most of the girls were light-skinned and quite pretty. We were sought after by gangsters, politicians, businessmen, anyone who was somebody. Some of these relationships resulted in marriage. And when they did, we never heard from our sister girlfriends again. So there were those who wanted to pass. But it was not for me and certainly not for Fredi or Adam.

I think that's one of the reasons I fell in love with Adam. He knew who he was. He was light enough to pass if he had wanted to, but he chose not to. That meant a lot to me and people of my complexion who are sometimes challenged about our blackness, not by whites but by other colored folk. It's not my fault if people can't see my blackness. I know who I am and what's in my heart.

Knowing how hard it is for colored people, Adam and I tried to reach out to help whenever we could. I had a colored maid, a little brown girl. She was from somewhere down South. It's a funny thing, but she seemed to resent working for me, another colored person. Now this gal, we took her to Oak Bluffs with us. We used to buy fresh-killed chickens. We would go over to the farm and have them killed. I would bring them home and then soak them in a little baking soda, to get the blood out. When she first came that summer, I would put the chickens in the baking soda and water and when I returned to the kitchen she had pulled it out of the water. She didn't cook, I cooked, so I asked her why.

The maid said, "Ms. Jr. Powell, who ever heard of soaking chickens in baking soda?" They used to call me Ms. Jr. Powell, they wouldn't call me Mrs. Powell. I guess the girl didn't know that I wasn't paying her for her opinion, but to do a job. I told her that's the way I wanted it and that's why I put the chickens in the water. I had that problem with some of the help. Finally I had to get a white maid, a little Scottish gal. For her, everything I wanted was fine. It didn't make any difference. If I had asked her to stand on her head, she would have done it. And, of course she called me Mrs. Powell.

Later I had another maid. She was from somewhere down South and had a mouth full of gold teeth. I would open my blinds in the morning and maybe go downtown. When I came back the blinds would be closed. I told her I left them open because I wanted the sun to come in. So I asked her why she closed the blinds. "Oh, that makes it too hot in here, Ms. Jr. Powell," she said. I really couldn't believe her. These are people I've gone out of my way to give work to and they won't even do the work according to my instruction. If a colored person has a colored boss, they have to treat that colored boss with the same respect that they would anybody else. These maids, for whatever reason, didn't do that. I would not tolerate their disrespect in my home so we let them go.

I believe that no matter what job you have, whether its pushing a broom or working in the telephone company, if a person works hard and does their best, they'll move up to better things. But first, the person has to do the job. Big Momma did laundry and took other odd jobs. She even did my friend Maude's laundry. The rent had to be paid come hell or high water and there was no welfare back then. I really couldn't believe that the maids I've mentioned had a hard time working for another colored person. I'm just as colored and proud with a black person as I am with a white person, maybe more with a colored person because they have an idea of what it took to get there.

Some people may find this hard to believe, but the same way that light-skinned blacks could pass, this whole fixation on color permitted whites of a certain hue to slip in going the other direction. If being colored were so horrible, you wouldn't have had any of this because people would have had too much pride in who they are. There were a few white girls performing at the clubs from time to time. Everyone knew they were white, but no one said anything. They were generally very nice because they didn't want their secret to get out. Their argument was that as a light-skinned colored woman, they were considered "fabulous." They preferred that to being an ordinary white woman. They were able to find work all the time. I guess when things got slow they could go back the other way or just perform until someone made an honest woman of them.

By the time the United States got into World War II, the nation was in a racial quandary. Colored people continued to assert themselves, demanding rights they had never had, but the troops remained segregated. It made no sense to us that we should fight for someone else's freedom when we were second-class citizens here at home.

Adam, Fredi and I were all against this type of hypocrisy. Even though Fredi had traveled extensively and entertained all over Europe, her heart was right here in America. She was downright mad but she didn't let it stop her patriotism. She was one of the first women to go get her an American Women's Voluntary Services (AWVS) uniform. The AWVS provided all kinds of support services for the war effort. The uniforms were a sort of blue-gray and very smart looking. Her picture appeared in the paper. In a column that she wrote for Adam's paper, *The People's Voice*, she talked about how grown up our nephew had become since joining the military and what a fine young man he was now. In another column she praised the War Department for finally letting colored performers go overseas and entertain the troops. She even called on some of the bigger names she knew like Paul Robeson, Hazel Scott, and Ethel Waters to forego their generous salaries and go over and entertain the troops.

As colored people in America, we never know when color will become an issue or how much of an issue. We might even be insulted, but sometimes we just let it go. My clothes were made by one of the deaconesses at the church. She made me this black suit one time. The top fastened in the back and there were black matching shorts. It was the cutest outfit. I was walking down Circuit Avenue, having come out of the drugstore. I used to take baby oil and a few drops of iodine and shake it up and rub it on my skin. This mixture gives the most gorgeous color. These two foreign white women passed me and they were milk white. They stared at me as they passed and one of them tapped me on the shoulder.

"Miss, excuse me ma'am, but how did you get that gorgeous color?" she asked me. I explained what I had done and told her to go right here indicating the drugstore and get her some baby oil and iodine. Finally she came back once more and asked, "But Miss, do you use this in the winter time?" In other words, she just wanted to look like that over here but when she returned home she wanted her regular color back. It was clear that she wanted to try the color on but not to look like that the rest of her life. There's a stigma.

Adam didn't care too much about stigmas. He invited the Communists to Harlem for some political rallies. They came to Harlem because they felt we were the most vulnerable and oppressed people in the country. We were ripe for the movement. They had placards and banners with catchy sayings. There were lots of blacks screaming and hollering when Paul Robeson who had the most gorgeous voice of his time addressed the people.

Adam was not a Communist, he was a politician. Our government associated him with the Reds so much so that my brothers were investigated when they left to serve their country in the military. Adam worked with the Communists because he believed in achieving real freedom for colored people and other oppressed groups by any means available. I believe he would have worked with the devil if the devil had promised true freedom for all. If America had lived up to its promise of freedom for the Negro, the Communists would never had gotten any place in Harlem.

Fredi was regarded as a suspect for a time too because she campaigned for racial, political, and economic equality. It made it very hard for her to get work or to be considered for the better acting roles. She wanted what all of us deserved, better and more opportunities!

CHAPTER 14

Gone Fishin

Years ago, Old Man Powell and Adam weren't the only leaders in the neighborhood with a vision for the Negro. At least two other movements gave them some type of competition. Anyone around at the time remembers Marcus Garvey parading down the street, sitting in his open car with his feathered hat, calling people back to Africa. He was short and round and had beautiful black skin. He preached Negro racial pride. He attracted large numbers of people who would also wear the plumed hats. He tried to address the needs of the poor but also encouraged education and professional training. People were so desperate for anything. Garvey gave the people of Harlem hope and that was more than some of the other charlatans out at the time gave them.

When Adam was younger, he had been fascinated by Garvey. Adam used to watch him talk and saw how other blacks reacted to him. He loved listening to his speeches because so few leaders even thought about black pride but it was Garvey's main theme. Adam never forgot the experience of listening to Garvey. He took those cherished lessons on racial pride everywhere he went. It became part of him and part of the message he took to the people. Other "prophets" of the day did little to inspire Adam and even less for Harlem.

When four little ones toddled down the aisle at Abyssinia one Sunday morning, I was in the middle of a song, but they touched my heart at its center. We were welcoming our new members. These were four of the raggediest little tots you've ever seen. It was winter time. They weren't wearing winter coats and their hair was disheveled. They had been left on the front stoop of the church with a note. The oldest was about seven. Their mother abandoned her children when she went to join Father Divine. His movement was what you might call a cult today. When you joined it, you gave up everything. We knew to stay away from groups like that but people really were truly desperate.

I got out of my seat and went to see about those kids. I grabbed their little hands, took them upstairs, and got them bathed and fed. We put them in little white robes someone made special for them. That night I went to visit their father. The four children were asleep on a single twin bed, no blanket, no sheet. Nearby was a small box that he fed pennies into to make the power work. He couldn't pay his electric bill.

The father told me how disheartened he was. I told him the church would do all it could to help. They could stop by the soup kitchen for a meal. I would personally see to it that they were fed and he could come by too. I took those babies under my wing and put them in my choir. The Tiny Tots Choir was for babies from two to twelve and the Junior Choir was for kids from twelve to sixteen. I was determined to make sure that these tiny tots had what they needed to grow up with Christian values and become somebody. I knew what it was like to grow up without a mother.

The church had a clothes bank and I made sure those little ones got a couple of decent outfits. People brought clothes by the church. However, the main thing was that people had no food. We continued with the food bank, and Adam also had ideas to add employment and discounted food.

By the time the weather began to change, the four children were doing much better and had actually made a few friends in the church. From time to time I saw them smile and laugh. It gave me such joy. And when they stretched their little arms around me to give me a hug, it made my heart sing. I prayed for the mother, that she would come to her senses and come back.

Every three months or so we had Choir Festival with all of the choirs including the Junior Choir, the Young People's Choir and the Men's Choir. It was such a blessing to hear all the choirs at once. I would sit up front and they would work hard to impress the pastor's wife, the Queen of Harlem. In addition to the choirs, I also did plays with the children. One of our deacons worked down at Radio City Music Hall and he used to give me all kinds of props and things and I'd have the men from church pick them up. We put on fabulous plays and awakened confidence and creativity in some of those kids that they never knew they had. Everyday I thanked God for what He had given me. I was not far removed from the theater. Even when I traveled with Adam, sometimes he would speak and

I would sing. I had the best of both worlds. I had left Broadway behind, but I was always on stage with Adam.

Our summer trips to the island were vacations from the heavy load at the church but not from the spotlight. Adam and I both rather enjoyed the attention but occasionally the rigidity of the church would annoy me. Oak Bluffs was my refuge. As the Fourth of July holiday approached, I prepared for the trip to the island. Adam and my brother Bubba used to go on fishing trips to Florida all the time. Sometimes I joined them, but this time Adam took off all alone and said he'd be back. He returned just in time to head to the island.

When we were on our honeymoon, we stayed at Shearer Cottage. Over the next few years, we rented a place for ourselves. But this time Adam wanted to come up with me. I didn't think anything of it other than he had a little more time off. He generally came on the weekends and couldn't spend too much time on the island because of his work at the church. When we got to Oak Bluffs, I just about cried. Bunny had bought us a cottage of our own. I was so surprised, I screamed with delight. It was just the most darling little get away you could imagine. We named it the Bunny Cottage. It had been part of a barn and had been brought over to this lot. Later they built an addition on to the house and transformed it into a cottage. Now we would really enjoy the summers, what with our own place and all. I would always remember the summer of 1936.

I told Adam and Bubba this house almost made up for them leaving me in a cast to go fishing in Florida a few years prior. I had gotten sciatica again. It would come and go. They'd take care of it and it would go. But this time it didn't go. The doctors didn't want to take any chances, they cut into my spine and put me back into a body cast. Adam and Bubba had planned this fishing trip for a long while. Bubba got time off from work and Adam only had but so many days off at the church. Of course they asked if I wanted them to stay. I was trying to be gracious and said that they could go. I would be right here when they got back in a few days. Fredi, Rosebud, Maude, and the others would surely help me out. I told them to go have fun and bring back some whoppers. Instead of staying at home, like I wanted them to do, they actually took off. They left me and went on down to Florida to fish. I couldn't believe it.

Once again, my clothes had to be made to accommodate the cast. I was really over a barrel. I couldn't do much around the house and was under doctor's orders not to move around if it wasn't necessary. They had to make sure my spine was okay. One night after Adam had returned, I got out of bed to go to the bathroom, fell, and couldn't get up. I was crying but I was so embarrassed, I wouldn't call Adam. He woke up and went looking for me. There I was, lying on the floor. He looked down asking, "Bunny, what are you doing down there?" I said, "I can't get up." He cracked up before lifting me up and helping me to the bathroom. After eight months we had a coming out party. The cast was placed on the banister and everybody who came signed the cast. The hospital also made a brace for me to wear when I went fishing.

Now that we had our own place, fishing on the island might be a little better than fishing in Florida. One of the first things I did was to invite the family up for a weekend. Fredi didn't come up too often. She usually had various jobs that kept her away. We only saw her occasionally. Rosebud came up more frequently. Bunny nicknamed us the Three Tittiless Wonders. Adam was very friendly with all of my family and most of my friends. He didn't have any problem with me hanging around former Cotton Club friends like Hycie Curtis and Maude Russell. He used to have great fun retelling the story of my breast pad coming out of my swimsuit.

Shortly after we got the house, Adam also got us a boat which we named "The Bunny." As soon as we could we went fishing in it. Hycie came up to visit. She had maintained her figure and was tall and thin. Adam wanted us to go to the bow of the boat and strike poses, just like the rich white girls, our hair blowing in the wind. Adam wanted every black person on the planet to know that they are just as good as any white person, that they should have the best, and deserved to be just as happy.

Adam was so proud of our cottage. He invited friends up at the drop of a hat. Church members and people who worked on his staff were invited too. We would entertain them royally and send them home with stories galore. With Adam it was a case of the more the merrier. I played the role of the dutiful hostess, cooking my specialties and making sure everyone enjoyed themselves. We would fish, go for walks on the beach, lunch at one of the places in town, and shop. In the evenings there were lovely dinners and cocktail parties.

I always had a great time when Maude came up to visit. I think of all my friends Adam may have liked her the best. They played around like sister and brother. We used to visit her when she lived on 80th and Nicholas Place in New York. We'd stop by with a few friends. Sometimes we'd eat hotdogs on Sunday nights late after church. We would actually play ball in the house with the hotdogs, throwing them back and forth across the room like school kids trying to hit one another. Then we'd wash them up real good, put them in the pot, boil them and eat them.

126

I never fed my guests hotdogs. If they made the effort to come all the way to the island, we either went out to dinner or I made them one of my gourmet meals. Unlike me, Maude hated to cook and would make any excuse to avoid having to torture herself in the kitchen. She would offer to do the dishes and could really keep some house, but no cooking. And that girl had an appetite on her. It's a wonder she was able to stay so thin.

Frequently Adam invited up close friends who were involved in politics. One weekend Joe Ford, a Southern politician, came up. We were all on the front porch of the Bunny Cottage talking about politics and what we could do to better conditions for the poor and oppressed. Both Joe and I had made a few suggestions and Adam had nodded his head. But when he began to speak again, I felt a tingle surge through my body. He walked up the porch and talked aloud as though he were giving a speech to himself. Then he looked off to the side at nothing in particular and affirmed to himself, "I'm going to run for Congress as the first black Congressman from the East. After a few terms, I'll return to New York and run for Governor or Senator."

"After that," he said, like he had just become aware that we were there, "Who knows?"

It was clear to us, he was thinking about the presidency in the distant future. He had it all mapped out. When we got a quiet moment alone, I brought up my reservations. Could he really serve the pulpit and constituents who *voted* him in at the same time? There might be conflicting interests and, with power, there would always be the possibility of corruption. I let him know that whatever he decided to do I was with him. I was his wife. But it was my duty to whisper these things into his ear so he could mull them over. My words of warning fell off his back like wrinkles in his jacket when he stood up.

We soon got to know our neighbors on the island, most of whom came up and spent the summers there. Dorothy West lived just a couple of houses away from our cottage. I knew that she wrote and had had some success during the Harlem Renaissance. We had been perfectly friendly to each other until a number of things started happening. She would rake leaves and leave them in other people's yards. She started talking about Adam, among other things calling him a playboy. She thought he liked her. My husband was unusually devoted to me and if he was doing anything behind my back, I would be the last to know. Frankly he was taking care of business at home. I didn't know Dorothy well, so I didn't trust her. Nor did I believe what she said.

As other things became an issue like the garbage and what

not, things that you share with neighbors, Dorothy and I went from friendly to "cordial." But we always spoke and greeted each other. Later she began to feed the birds, pigeons. They would crap at the side of our house. I had to have the wood replaced four times. And they had to shovel all the crap away before they could replace the wall. Then she got the bright idea to put bread crumbs down my way, in my bushes and near my flowers. She started feeding the crows and they made a lot of noise. Once I even caught her in the act. She hadn't seen me coming up so she was startled. I said, "Dorothy, what are you doing putting those bread crumbs out here for the crows?" She couldn't even find the words to respond. I don't know where the pigeons went but she didn't want those noisy crows down by her. If I see them and there's a stone nearby, I pick it up and throw it at them and tell them to go back down there to her house where they belong.

Dorothy had a cousin named Abby. Abby and I were considering a project. When a neighbor called Dorothy to ask about her cousin, Dorothy responded, "Oh, isn't she dead yet," referring to me. The Heavenly Father permitted me to outlive Dorothy and for that I am grateful. At first I didn't want to go to her funeral because of the unfriendly relationship we had. I didn't want to be hypocritical. Then I listened to wise counsel and I went because it was the gracious, the right thing to do. To my surprise, I got a standing ovation at her funeral.

On October 9th, 1943, another issue of Adam's paper, *The People's Voice* came out. Fredi was on vacation so I filled in and wrote her Headlines/Footlights column. I was thrilled. There was a little picture of me and Bunny up at Oak Bluffs. We had gone fishing and he hadn't caught a thing. I on the other hand was pulling them in like candy. When he demanded we change spots, I still caught fish and left him with only worms on his hook. I wrote about the fact that I had outfished him and he wanted to make excuses. It just couldn't be that I was better at fishing than him.

By now the United States was involved in World War II, and my baby, Preston had joined the Navy. I didn't know when he'd be able to get back to New York. Adam had taught him how to crab and cast a line and so many things a son learns from his father. I knew that I was truly blessed because of the warm relationship the two of them had. It was about 1944 and Adam suggested that I go up and visit Pres as I called him. Naturally I wanted to go see my son but I needed someone to travel with. Adam had just the right person, he suggested Maude. She happened to be free so off we went.

We headed for Chicago. Pres was at boot camp near the Great Lakes. I couldn't believe my baby was a sailor. I just prayed that he wouldn't be sent out of the country. If he stayed in the States chances are that he wouldn't get hurt. The train ride seemed to take forever, but I was laughing the whole way with Maude in the car. I really hadn't traveled much so when we got to Chicago and had to stay overnight in one of those little cheap hotels, I was glad to take a load off my feet. Maude wouldn't hear of it. She said, "Wait a minute, just a minute!" as though I were about to jump into a pigsty. She got out her cleaning gloves and her disinfectant and she went to work. She told me not to touch a thing as these little side of the road hotels were dirty. She even washed the doorknob and scrubbed out the bathtub. She cleaned all the chairs with disinfectant. Finally she was done. Thank God, because my legs were about to give out.

When we got to the base, Pres was tickled to death. He was so happy to see us. We had brought him some spareribs and he was ready to chow down cause the food on the base was not the best. But his Lieutenant ate nearly all of the ribs. Pres was upset but he couldn't say anything because that man outranked him.

After we left Pres, I headed back to the island and prepared for another set of visitors. Before they arrived, Adam told me all about the meetings I had missed in the council. As it got dark, we decided to go fishing. We went out in our boat, chasing striped bass. We used to send off the island for these blood worms. They fly them in and the fish love them. The fish have soft lips and no teeth so when they bite, they can suck the worm off the hook almost without you feeling it. We got on the boat and there was a black out as it still wartime. No lights at night. If the enemy wanted to attack us, they would have a hard time seeing the target. That's what we were told.

We went on down off the bridge where the fish go to the inlet to feed. In about twenty minutes, they had taken every bit of those two dozen worms and gone on about their business. So we turned around to come back. It was dark, I could hear the boat sloshing in the water, and I was just a little scared even with my big strong man guiding the boat. I thought it was a good idea to be prepared for anything, so I had gotten all of the life preservers and was lying down on deck. Adam was at the tiller, but it was dark and we struck a buoy. We were about two miles off shore, and the front of the boat rose up when it hit the buoy.

I had all the life preservers on me. I jumped up and Adam cut the boat right into shore. He didn't realize how badly damaged the boat was. It could have sunk right out there. Fortunately, we made it back safely. When we got home Adam said, "Bunny, nice one you were. When I looked, you had every one of those life preservers on you. You had two on each leg, two on each shoulder and I had none." I turned to him and said, "I can paddle, but you can swim! You weren't going to have another great American tragedy here."

He responded, "Well, you certainly fixed it up. I see you didn't intend to drown. If I had to drown, you were going to say you drown, but I'm gonna be saved cause I'm gonna be bobbing. No way I can go down with all these preservers on me." We had a good laugh about that one.

On one of the last times we took the Bunny out that summer, the motor stopped on us. We were really out there in the deep, right off from the lighthouse. I could see a young girl there. We weren't even able to drop anchor, right off from East Chop. All the fishing boats had passed us and gone in. I was getting scared. Of course, I was wearing my life preservers. This time I let Adam have a couple too. I tried to make him bring the boat in because a storm was coming up, but he was being stubborn. He kept saying, "No, we're going to catch the last fish and go on a little bit longer."

The boat was just rocking like it was dancing to music. For a moment I wondered if Adam saw what I saw, or if he was crazy. It was just all a little too macho for me. The anchor wouldn't hold because the water was so rough. Nothing Adam did would restart the boat. Finally, he got on top of the motor and with his big booming voice he started hollering, "HELP! HELP!" He yelled toward the lighthouse. The young woman we had seen ran out. "Help is coming!," she shouted. When the Coast Guard came to get us they had to throw us a line. They put us in tow and brought us in. Now every time I pass the lighthouse I think about that incident and the young woman who saved us. When they came and got us and I stepped on dry land, I was never so happy in my life. I told Adam that I was never going out there again. He said, "Oh yes, you are. We've got to turn around and go back." Against my better judgment, eventually I did go back out there. Fortunately, though, there were no more macho man incidents in the water with Adam while we fished.

CHAPTER 15

The Shadow of Washington

After returning from the island, we'd settle in and get ready for the holidays as the weather turned cool. The time always passed so quickly. As soon as we put up the tree and decorations at the church, Christmas was already knocking at our door. It became our holiday family tradition that Preston would play the violin while we all drank eggnog. I would sing Silent Night or another holiday carol and at the stroke of twelve midnight we'd stop and open our gifts. Old Man Powell would read a passage from the Bible. I so looked forward to this time each year, to spend private time with my family and thank God for His many blessings.

As usual, early one Sunday morning, Adam got up and wrote his sermon. He came back with our morning coffee and we discussed the activities for the day. When church was over we walked down Seventh Avenue to 125th Street. It was our normal routine for a Sunday morning, except it was different, much more exciting. This time Adam was running for Congress. I was right at his side. Adam had managed to avoid short changing the church while he was on the City Council, but if he were elected to Congress he'd have to spend a lot of time in Washington, D.C. That would be tricky. And we would have to raise money for his campaign.

This Sunday I wore my favorite outfit, a blue taffeta tucked skirt, wide, with a tiny little tight bodice and a high neck. I wore my matching blue straw hat that was covered in violets. It was the most beautiful outfit. Adam wore tails and striped pants and we made a stunning pair. As usual, he shook everyone's hand and greeted his constituents. On the corner of 125th Street, there was a diamond merchant. Adam went in to ask for a donation. The merchant told Adam he had a deal for him. He said Adam could either have $1,000 or diamonds he thought Adam might like. He brought out the diamonds and told Adam a story.

"There was a very wealthy Jewish man in Germany during the war, a millionaire. They took virtually everything from him but he did get out of Germany. The only thing he was able to bring with him was this." The merchant held up these incredible diamonds. The man had hidden them in cotton in his rectum and that's how he brought them out. He had brought them to the dealer who made Adam the offer. After he heard the story, Adam took the diamonds.

I'll never forget the day he brought them home and showed them to me. He offered them all to me but I said, "Look, I don't want to be greedy." He said, "Bunny, you know what you can do? You can have a ring made. You can break them down. You can have other jewelry made." I replied, "No, well let me think about it."

Not long after, we had a dinner engagement at the Governor's mansion. His wife had diamonds on every finger. I thought to myself what horrible taste. After that, I sent two of the diamonds back and kept the smallest one. I do wish someone would give me that offer today, I'd keep them all. We had the diamond set into a beautiful ring and kept right on campaigning.

During the election campaign, there was a political rally at a church near 116th Street, a little Baptist place between Park Avenue and Lexington. The mayor got there just before Adam. Adam came up quickly in front of the mayor to address the small crowd. He said, "I'm the mayor and you will have to wait until the finish!" The people fell out laughing. Adam looked over at the mayor and kept laughing himself.

We campaigned and talked to people until we were hoarse and our toes fell off. We left no stone unturned and made sure everyone knew he was running and what he stood for. Adam had entered the race with the confidence of a tiger. Sure enough, several months later when the results came in, he had won! We were so excited and I was so proud of my Bunny Boy. Once again I let him know that I was behind him but was concerned about his political ambitions in relation to his religious duty. I was also concerned about the effect this would have on our marriage. When I brought this up, Adam pretended that it was a non-issue. But you don't live with someone for eleven years and not understand how their ego works.

All of us were happily exhausted from the campaign. We had earned a few days of rest. Adam had worked so hard that it affected his health. He was under doctor's orders to rest, so we went up to the cottage at Oak Bluffs for a few days. It was nice and cool and the breezes off the water helped me to clear my head of all of the campaign rigamarole. I began to relax and Adam and I took walks down by the water. It was absolutely beautiful to watch the sunset.

I began to focus on the huge job of moving us to Washington, D.C. There would be so much to organize and pack. I'd have to find the right kind of place to live. And I would need a slightly different wardrobe to fit in with the sophisticated Washington wives. A magazine had done a fashion piece about a Congressman's wife. She had a pair of Airedale puppies and was photographed walking her pets.

One evening I asked Adam if I could get a brace of Airedales. I thought they would help me fit in better. We had just come in from one of our walks and Adam was smoking his ever lit pipe. I picked up the magazine to show him the picture. We were in the living room in front of a large mirror. Adam's response literally left me speechless.

In a slow, calm, but unsteady voice, he managed to say, "Bunny, I love you more than anything in the world, but you won't be needing the dogs. You won't be going to Washington with me."

My body began to panic. I dropped the magazine on the floor, and fell back on the sofa as my heart began to race. I wasn't exactly sure what he meant. Or maybe he was playing some kind of joke as he loved to do. He placed his hands on my shoulders. I was facing the mirror and glanced at his back. When I looked into his eyes, he turned away.

"What?" is all I could manage to get out of my throat.

When he turned his back on me and left the room, I knew this was no joke. After all we had been through. After all I had done for him, for the church, because I was his wife. I couldn't believe that he could even think about leaving me. He couldn't just walk out like nothing had ever happened between us. How dare he. I called after him, but he kept moving away.

"Bunny, what about sex?" "Oh, you can always be celibate," he turned to answer me.

His response was cruel. Now I was mad and I knew he wasn't fooling. But when he said those words I wanted to collapse to the floor. When had he stopped caring about me? How had I let him down? This could not be happening to me. Adam was the pastor of a church! He couldn't just decide to ditch his wife! I still loved him. Why was he doing this to me, to us?

I cried out, "But why?" My throat was very dry and I could hardly swallow. I could barely talk. "I have to move on because I've outgrown you. I need to move forward and you want to stand still," he said, throwing his words at me like darts. I didn't know what to say. I didn't know what to do. My husband had just been elected to Congress and he was going to leave me? No!

I couldn't eat. I couldn't sleep. In fact, I couldn't function at all. For two whole weeks I ate nothing and cried all the time. The thought of food was repulsive and made me nauseous. Occasionally I managed to swallow small amounts of water. I thought I had the answer – suicide. If I killed myself then it would end this nightmare and I wouldn't be in all of this pain. I could not live without Adam. He was my life. As I considered suicide, I knew I had to do something, talk to somebody. I did the only thing left that I knew how to do. I called Fredi and Maude. Both were in town, and Fredi came right away.

It didn't take long for news of our pending divorce to spread. Mayor La Guardia came by the parsonage to see me. I wouldn't see most people, but I saw him. He patted me on the back and told me everything would be all right. His visit was appreciated.

Adam swooped in with Old Man Powell and his lawyers. I felt under attack by the man who had promised to love me forever. They actually wanted me to leave my home, the private residence on St. Nicholas Avenue that the church had purchased for us to live in, the parsonage. I refused, almost daring them to kick me out, to evict the First Lady of Abyssinia. I went from anger to depression, to self-pity, to suicidal and back again. I didn't know what to think or what to feel. I thought if I agreed to what they wanted, Adam would change his mind and come back to me. How do you just wake up one morning and stop loving your spouse? How could he leave me like this and why? I didn't have an existence without him.

Fredi came in and took over. Thank God for my sister. Maude and her husband recommended a lawyer. I couldn't do anything for myself. Fredi took me to a doctor who gave me some sort of shot to make me eat. I have never been a heavy person to begin with so two weeks of not eating just about made me disappear. I lost fourteen pounds. I thought Abyssinia was a place that I could trust, where I could remain for the rest of my life. Surely the church would come to my rescue. I was wrong, still the outsider that I had been when I first arrived, that church turned me out like a complete stranger they had never known. It was clear who they were devoted to, their pastor who was now on his way to Congress. I filed for separation as I became aware of the nasty rumors that Adam was seeing Hazel.

When we went to court, the case was dismissed because neither of us had shown up to address the charges. His lawyers had contacted us and wanted to talk. Fredi selected lawyers and arranged everything. I was in a deep depression but no longer wanted to take my own life. Fredi got all of my things out of the parsonage because I didn't know left from right or which way was up. She was so mad at Adam, she could hardly stand to be in the same room with him.

Finally, the lawyers came to some kind of agreement. I was to go to Reno and file for divorce. Why did they want *me* to "divorce" him when he was the one who was unfaithful? I cannot repeat in these pages the language Fredi used with Adam, his father, and his lawyers. Not even a sailor would use such words. Adam had his secretary make an inventory of everything in our apartment, even down to the number of rolls of toilet paper. Fredi thought the way Adam had done this, it had been carefully planned. I didn't care. I just wanted the pain to stop. I wanted my Bunny back.

Once I began to accept the fact that Adam was leaving me for good, that he wasn't going to change his mind, Fredi suggested that I take back my maiden name of Washington. "The name 'Washington' is just as prestigious as the name 'Powell,'" she said. I wouldn't hear of it. It wasn't just the name, it was the man behind the name, my Bunny Boy. She knew and everyone else knew that, even though we were divorcing, I was still in love with him.

Now that I was trying to prepare for life without Adam, I had to find a place to live. Maude was the first person I asked. I really needed her now. I came right out after a few minutes and asked if I could live with her. She tried to make me laugh as she always did and I managed a light chuckle. But she gave me all the excuses in the world why I couldn't come live with her. It seemed odd at the time, but later on I understood. We were such good friends, more like sisters, and if I came to live with her then our friendship might not survive.

She would do anything in the world for me but she didn't think living with her would be the best thing right now. She made a joke about how difficult I was to live with. I didn't find the joke funny at all. It felt like a hot slap in the face from my best friend. But Maude was right. I went to live with another friend right after my divorce and the friendship just didn't survive. Thank God I had Maude.

It burned me up that Old Man Powell was finally getting his way. After over eleven years of marriage, Adam and I would be divorced. I heard from friends that he approved of the union between Adam and Hazel. He thought she had class, that she was worldly and sophisticated. Never mind the fact that Adam was a pastor involved in an adulterous affair. Maybe Old Man Powell thought it was okay because he wasn't faithful to Mother Powell either, like father, like son. Class or no class, it would not end well because of how it began. I returned to church one last time to say goodbye to some friends. When I ran into Satan and Satan Jr., boy did I hightail it out of there. I was so angry and so hurt I thought I might explode.

There were so many people who didn't want Adam to marry me. But together we had overcome all the naysayers and made it. His father had never been able to stand me, and just when I thought he had finally come around and fully accepted me as his daughter-in-law, wham, Adam hits me with this. At least Old Man Powell had stopped calling me Jezebel. The same deacons and parishioners who turned their noses up at me would later welcome Hazel. What happened to the Commandment against adultery? Oh, there were a few who held out and said it was wrong, but they were in the minority because Abyssinia loooooved it some Adam. He could do no wrong.

After he had graduated from Colgate and gone on to the New York City Union Theological Seminary, the president of the institution told Adam directly that he disapproved of his relationship with me. Like his father, the president tried to persuade Adam to leave me. But Adam was his own man and thought his choice of a woman was none of the president's business. Adam thought about leaving the place then but stayed because he wanted the credential. All he had previously was the degree from Colgate. But there was some tension left in the air. When Adam got back a prayer paper with a poor mark, he was furious. He thought that the president had no right to tell him his conversation with God was of no use. No man had the right to make such a judgment. That was enough for Bunny, he left that place.

Mother Powell had always liked me. She was very upset by what Adam was doing. We were close and I believe she really valued my friendship. Old Man Powell was not always nice to her and, yes, there had been some indiscretions. He was also fond of drinking hard liquor. There was no one there for her to share her pain with. But I was there, and I could see the pain in her face. She took solace in my being there.

When she passed away, Adam was truly broken. He had recently announced our divorce. On Sunday he spoke at church. The divorce was on everyone's lips. He said no one could leave the church, that he had FBI agents at all the doors. He told them that he was going to tell them something and demanded that no one dare get up and leave. The "battle" between Adam and I, and how it should turn out was the topic of discussion everywhere, including the tabloids. He even accused the congregation of killing his mother by actively participating in this gossip.

When Mother Powell passed away, it was like a poison arrow

striking me, removing any possibility of recovery for our marriage. If anyone wanted us to stay together, it was Mother Powell, and even though he didn't always do what she wanted, Adam listened to his mother. He adored her. He was absolutely heartbroken when she died. I could only watch from a distance, knowing that she wouldn't want this. She had doted on him his entire life, but she had also told him when he was wrong. I was as heartbroken as Adam because Mother Powell had become like a mother to me. She taught me many things that a daughter can only learn from a mother who has already been there, done that, and knows how it will turn out. She had opened her arms wide and welcomed me into her family.

There was a club at the church named for her, the Mattie Fletcher Powell Club. It raised funds for senior citizen homes. When we made our first quilt, we had raised about twenty five hundred dollars. That was a large sum of money in those days. People paid to have their names put on the quilt, which was entirely handmade. The names closest to the center paid the most money. The club gave me the quilt after the money had been raised. It was a kind and loving gesture. It was such an honor for me to receive that quilt. I still treasure it to this day.

Mother Powell had been sick for a while before she finally passed on. But years before, when she was still healthy, she had toured Europe and had been entertained by a number of celebrities, including Josephine Baker and Bricktop. She was a quiet and demure woman, but sophisticated and loved by many.

CHAPTER 16

Train Drunk

Eleven years. We had been married for eleven joyous and full years. We had done everything together. Adam gave me a special set of dishes made in Europe to celebrate our anniversary. I fixed him a gourmet meal and we made love. The factory where the dishes were made had been burned down during the war. We had even gone to Café Society to hear *that* woman play. How could he do this to me? How could I have been such a fool? I thought we were happy. Like all marriages, we certainly had our problems, but this – a divorce, we had never even been separated. Adam couldn't possibly be serious. This was just some kind of phase my Bunny was going through. He was a Congressman now. He needed more space, more time, more love, more understanding. The cottage on the vineyard, what would happen to that? Adam absolutely loved to fish. I know there were other places, but nothing was like Oak Bluffs. Nothing made sense to me right now.

No matter what questions I asked myself, the answer was always wrong. I didn't know how he could do this to me, his Bunny Girl – the one he loved so much, the one he defied his father for, the one he gave up the church for. And I had given up my life for him. What was I supposed to do now? I certainly couldn't go back to the stage now, not after twelve years of domestication, working with Tiny Tots, and putting on kiddie plays. Broadway would laugh at me. Even if I used my show business age, I'd still be too old.

I tore up the love letters and gave away all of the perfume. I would have torn up the photographs too but I began to look at them. When the memories came flooding back and the emotions swept me away, I just couldn't manage to rip them apart. I had to put them away for a while so I wouldn't be reminded so often of him. It was bad enough that we lived in the same part of the city, and had many mutual friends.

When I vowed before God and three thousand witnesses at Abyssinia Baptist Church to love and cherish Adam until death do us part, I meant it. I had always thought of him as my knight in shining armor. It took me a long time to realize that he was a man, a mortal, just like every other man, with strengths and weaknesses, no matter what he wore on the outside, linen suits, steel armor, or even a pastor's robe.

Fredi wrote me a note and said not to open it until the train left Newark. She hugged me tight as she put me on the train. The doors to the drawing room were wide open. The room was bedecked with flowers, every color and variety under the sun. All the porters from here to Chicago knew my business. They knew all about it. It was in all of the papers and even on some of the radio programs. There was no place for me to hide, no privacy anywhere. I was headed out west to file for divorce as agreed.

Just as the train was leaving, the porter said to me, "Now Mrs. Powell, there's a bell right there. If anything happens and you need me, just ring and I'll be right here." I nodded my head. I was sitting there by myself in the middle of all those flowers. As the train began to pull out, I began to cry. I was leaving behind my life with Adam and I would no longer be Mrs. Adam Clayton Powell Jr.

This old white drunk saw me and stumbled right into my room. He sat down beside me. His speech was slurred. He looked and smelled like he had been drinking for several days.

He asked, "What's the matter with the poor pretty little lady? Who died?"

"Get out, get out!" I said trying to muster some force into my voice.

"No cause I know you're sad," he said. I must have really looked pretty pathetic for a drunkard to feel sympathy for me.

I didn't know what this drunk thought he could do to help me, but I reached over and called the porter. When the porter looked in and saw the drunk he dragged him out. I stared at the flowers until the train pulled in to Newark. How could they be so beautiful and happy when I was so low and miserable? Some people got off the train and a bunch of people got on. When the train started moving again, I opened the letter Fredi had written to me.

Dear Belle:

You are embarking on a new life. The future is in front of you. The past is behind you. Never look over your shoulder.

And I never have, never have. Fredi, Sister, my big sister, she was always there when I needed her and God how I needed her now. If it hadn't been for Fredi I really don't know what I would have done. I closed my eyes and inhaled the mixed fragrance of the flowers. It smelled like spring. Then I starred at the colorful blooms trying to count the petals on each one. I drank coffee but ate very little.

The train stopped in Chicago and I got up to stretch my legs. The next thing I knew there was a reporter asking me questions and taking notes. I couldn't let him see that side of me, the side that wanted to weep and wallow. It just wasn't proper to put your private business out in the street. I decided to go ahead with the interview. I spoke with the *Chicago Defender* and explained that my husband was a "devoted father," and a "perfect husband." I told them like I tell everybody else. He was good to me. I was hoping to get people off my back.

My picture was in the paper announcing my arrival in town. An announcer had mentioned it on a radio program too. Walter Winchell, *the* gossip columnist, came on the air every Sunday night. He kept mentioning my name as though he had an investigator following me around. Couldn't they find any better news to report than my business? When I got off the train, the media was standing there, waiting. They took some pictures before I was whisked away as fast as possible.

I stayed with a friend at a private residence. For days I moped around the house like a long-faced sad puppy. Occasionally, the edges of my lips turned up when I grimaced at the sun on my daily walk down the dirt path to check the mailbox. The sun felt good on my back, but there was nothing else good about my life right now. Fredi called to check on me regularly. She knew I was going to be okay. If I had just a little of her confidence, I could make it through the rest of the day. All I could do was take it one day at a time.

When the phone rang the next day, I thought it might be Fredi, Preston, or Maude calling to check on me, but it was actually someone from the United States government asking me to entertain the troops at one of the camps. I was embarrassed that they had even asked me. Why, I hadn't been in show business for over ten years except for a radio program. Then I told myself, why not? If they wanted me to I would do it. I would put my grief aside for the boys, yes. It was something for me to do, other than think about my divorce.

I put on one of my sharpest outfits and made up my face. They came and picked me up and put me in one of those little jeeps and drove me all around the base. I saw all the young men and they were so wonderful to me. I was bouncing up and down in that thing. They tried hard to make me happy, to help me forget my troubles. I was so scared that my voice would crack as I tried to sing, but once the music started it was as if I had never stopped performing. I sang a few songs and they rewarded me with thunderous applause. For the rest of the time I was in Vegas, the men would drop by where I was staying to leave me gifts, flowers and candy. I was pleased with myself. I had done my civic duty. Now I was like Fredi.

In the midst of my own debacle, my heart went out to the troops. Alonso, my eldest brother, had gone to the Army, while most of the men in the family had gone to the Navy. These men risked their lives for us so the least I could do was put on a happy face for them. Like a clown at a party, I put on a smile and a shimmie and made like life was wonderful and this was a great place. When I got back to my room, I wiped off the smile like bad make-up, but just thinking about the laughter and smiles on those soldiers' faces made me feel better.

Now that I was feeling a little bit better, I decided to give Adam one last chance. On the first day of the hearing, if he wanted to put all of this behind us, I would let him. I knew my Bunny Boy would come around. He would do the right thing. We still loved each other.

However, on the day of the hearing, I found out just what kind of man Adam was. The hearing was private, and the judge was not fond of Adam or his petty excuses. Bunny sashayed in with his father and three lawyers. Adam fought to give up as little as possible, claiming that he could only afford but so much. I knew that Adam had the money to live as lavish a lifestyle as he wanted. I watched and listened in wonder as Adam and his lawyers tried to deceive the judge. Several times I had to stop myself from walking out of the room. I wondered if the nasty rumors were true, that he was sleeping with Hazel Scott, who we called the boogie woogie pianist. Would she be his next victim?

I listened to Adam and his lawyers, hoping that none of it was true. By the time we finished I was sick to my stomach and I knew that it was all true. I felt like the biggest fool. This was the man that I had given my heart to, that I had given up my career for. I had been a star on Broadway on my way to the top. I had had church up to my ears, Baptist and Catholic, but I had put those feelings aside because I loved this man so. Now I had no way to earn a living and he couldn't *afford* to take care of me? What nonsense.

Fredi and I sat on one side of the chambers and Adam, and his father, and his lawyers sat on the other side. We faced the judge ready for war. My lawyers fought just as hard as his. And since the judge didn't fall for his act, I came away with a modest settlement which included the deed to the Bunny Cottage on Martha's Vineyard. When we left the room, I couldn't believe it was over, just like that.

For a long time I was furious at Adam for what he had done to me, to us. I had trusted him with all my heart. I had given up my first love for him. He had ruined my life and still I couldn't find it in me to hate him. I didn't realize that when Adam quit a woman he quit them for good. He would have nothing to do with me ever again. Maude used to say that he was as cold as a Norwegian turd. Maybe she was right.

When I saw that he had married Hazel Scott, I hated her. Adam and I had actually gone to Café Society to hear her play several times. Adam had also taken my little sister down there so he could sneak and see Hazel. Even at her young age, my sister knew something was funny between Adam and Hazel. When Rosebud told me about it, I paid her no mind. She was too young to understand how devoted Adam was to me. Apparently, Hazel would come over to their table giggling like a teenager. Then she'd come to church the next day and pretend nothing was going on.

Even Old Man Powell got in on the act. He took my sister aside, resting his hands on her shoulders. "You're too young to understand these things now, but Adam wants a son. When you get older, you're going to understand these things."

And to think, Hazel Scott was having an affair with my husband. I certainly was the last to know. I trusted him so much that if he had done something right in front of me, I would have doubted my own eyes. I was stupid or blinded by love or both. I was too caught up in the Cinderella lifestyle and title of Mrs. Adam Clayton Powell Jr.

More than anything, I hated Hazel because she gave Adam the one thing I couldn't, a child. I guess he wanted an heir more than he wanted our marriage. When she gave birth to a boy, right around the time that our divorce became final, I knew there was very little chance of him coming back. I thought about my second pregnancy and how I had wished it would just end. I didn't know if it was something I had done before, or the terrible incident with the horse, but after all those years of marriage, I never became pregnant. I would have literally done almost anything in this world to have had a child with my husband, but it was too late. There would be no diamond anniversary celebration.

I comforted myself with one of Big Momma's sayings, that "God don't like ugly and He would take care of everything." I was surprised to learn that Big Momma had been married several times. When her husbands didn't threat her well, she asked God to move them and He did. She told me not to worry and did everything she could to support and encourage me. I wondered if she could beat some sense into Adam with Dr. Black Pill, but the doctor had long since retired and could not be revived. Contrary to her usual prediction of gloom, she told me that the world was *not* coming to an end. But this time I disagreed with her. "Oh, no Big Momma, this time it is." The world coming to an end was the only way to survive this mess.

Adam's new relationship was doomed from the beginning. A woman couldn't smile in my face, commit adultery, come to church acting holier than thou, steal my husband, and expect to go on like nothing had happened. Of course, they were both wrong. But she knew not to mess with a married man.

Almost from the time we had started dating, women had lusted after Adam. I saw it in the way they looked at him, the way they smiled at him, how they held onto his hand for minutes when a simple handshake was appropriate. And the women at the church were just ridiculous. From showing their underwear, to sitting right up front wearing revealing clothing, and jumping up with a "Hallelujah and Amen," before Adam even had a chance to speak. They offered to do anything, and I mean anything at all, to assist in whatever he wanted done. I thought none of that meant anything because he was M-A-R-R-I-E-D! But maybe his marital status attracted women even faster. One of the reasons I became very active in the church is that I didn't want all of these women spending hours with my husband and me not being anywhere nearby. I needed to know what was going on. If I didn't know Adam, I did know women.

While I was in the middle of trying to figure out my life, a new guy had come into town. He had come here to become a star. He wanted to know all about show business and if we could take him around a little. He sang and played the piano. He was short, handsome, and very talented. I thought he was a bit naïve, but I saw some of the determination in him that I used to have. He had endless energy. I left my grief at home and went to meet with this guy. He had no idea that I was going through a divorce and felt absolutely miserable. Why should he, he had stars in his eyes. His name was Bobby Short. Fredi took him around mostly, but I shared what little knowledge I had that I thought might be of value to him. When I returned home, there was my grief waiting for me like an old friend. It was almost a comfort, I was getting so used to it.

Though it was very hard for me, I wished Adam and Hazel well. I still loved my Bunny Boy but I understood that he was human like everybody else, with lots of frailties. I followed his career and hoped he would do for the United States Congress and the world what he had accomplished for New York – full civil rights in more nooks and crannies than we even knew existed. He was still a political champion and I hoped he would win every fight. But surely he knew that this was not the way to begin his first session in Congress.

The Daughters of the American Revolution (DAR) declined Hazel's application for a concert at Constitution Hall in Washington, D.C. That's exactly the type of thing that would set Adam off. He wrote to Mrs. Truman hoping that the First Lady would resign from the DAR as Eleanor Roosevelt had done on behalf of Marian Anderson. But Mrs. Truman was no Mrs. Roosevelt. Adam organized a media campaign depicting Mrs. Truman as the Last Lady of the Land which President Truman did not look fondly upon. The President effectively black-listed Adam and his new wife. Adam kept right on fighting, so did his adversaries. Some of them included in the Congressional Record defenses of Mrs. Truman and comments about how horribly Adam had treated me, his first wife. I did not appreciate defenses of this type which were politically motivated.

I watched from a distance the various attacks on Bunny, knowing in my heart that his first few years in Congress would have been very different had we stayed together. With each incident he appeared to become more and more outspoken as though he thought he was invincible.

Prior to our divorce, Adam and Fredi got along wonderfully. I was pleased that my husband got along well with the sibling who practically raised me. It made everything so much easier. Of course tension at the paper increased until Fredi could no longer tolerate working for anything connected to Adam. She left after a couple years.

CHAPTER 17

On My Own

When I woke up and found out I was no longer the grand dame, so to speak, with a chauffeur, a maid, and a this and a that, it was traumatic. I was in shock. I still had the summer home. I got that in my divorce proceedings. But each morning I'd get up and make my coffee, put it in my silver coffee pot and go back to bed and sip it there. Habits die hard. It took me time to adjust, a long time. I knew the change was there and it had to be, but *I* never changed.

Fredi had to teach me how to make out a check. I had never paid a bill before. When I arrived on the island, my menus were made out by Adam's secretary. He made them out, what he wanted, and they were put on the pantry door near the kitchen. My soaps and everything were ordered from Bloomingdales. I appreciated not having to concern myself with the little things so I could devote my attention to cooking, entertaining, supporting my husband, and keeping myself looking good. Adam liked it that way. But I did it for myself too. Even now, I don't come downstairs without applying my make-up and lipstick.

I found a place of my own. I lived with my sister Rosebud but I didn't want to wear out my welcome. My family was very understanding. When Adam and I were together they had always been welcome. Now the shoe was on the other foot. Harlem was my home, like a favorite pair of shoes that might need replacing, but are so comfortable that you keep wearing them. So I stayed. Adam and I had walked past the apartment together a number of times during our strolls. The place had not been long built. A sign was swinging from the top so everybody could see it. The sign read FOR

WHITES ONLY. Adam remarked, "Will you look at that?" It was the kind of thing that set him off. Now, I've lived in that very same building for well over fifty years. At least some things have changed for the better.

Sometimes my younger siblings had come to stay with me and Adam during the weekends. They had loved meeting all the big names and going to the fancy places that you had to be eighteen to get into. And when the chauffeur drove them anywhere, they were in seventh heaven. I looked around my one bedroom apartment. There was barely enough room for me, let alone from other people. I didn't have much to offer my siblings any more, but I was sure glad to have them. I would need everybody to get through this thing. Words did not exist to describe what he had done to me, and I could find no words to express how I felt.

After twelve years with Adam, there was no coffee or drug strong enough to lift me out of my depression. Once I understood that I could live without him, I staggered through the demands of everyday life like a zombie. Had it not been for my family and friends, there's no way I would have made it. I was so deeply hurt, it felt like a mortal wound. And everyone I knew was absolutely disgusted with Adam.

Big Momma was especially disappointed. She went back to her old church and stopped attending Abyssinia. She reminded me that God does answer prayers, that I was always in hers and that He could heal my heart if I would let Him.

Fredi and Bubba encouraged me to get over Adam. He was the loser, they said. He would never have anybody as good as me that loved him like I had so it was his loss. He had married a beautiful top of the line Cotton Club dancer and Broadway star, who was sought after by any number of men, *he* had been the lucky one, not me. I should just get over him and move on with my life. They wouldn't have it any other way. Fredi reminded me to keep up my make-up and that I was still a lovely young woman who deserved the very best. Bubba did everything a big brother could to console me. Rosebud was there for moral support. As the baby of the family, she didn't offer much advice, but I was so glad to have her there. By this time, Preston had married and had two kids, Tommy and Tia whom he brought to see me. My grandchildren were so precious to me, but still I was unable to bring myself out of this fog, to let go.

Maude had an entirely different take on things. Even after the divorce, she thought it was better to be with him than to be alone. But since I was alone, I should carry myself in a certain manner and hold my head up. I had done nothing wrong and there was nothing for me to be ashamed of. She stopped going to Abyssinia too.

With their almost daily doses of encouragement, family and friends were constantly calling to check on me. They brought me plates of food even though I had no appetite.

Sometimes they would insist that I sit right down and eat the food while they were there to make sure it didn't end up in the trash. They would help me tidy up the place and vacuum. The apartment was hardly ever without flowers or plants that someone brought. I sincerely appreciated and loved them for everything they did, but somewhere in my heart and soul, I just needed to be alone. I had to grieve. It wasn't for a physical person, but for my marriage that had died. Born March, 1933 – Deceased July, 1945. But the vow said til death do you part. Both of us were very much alive. It wasn't right.

It took me a full year to begin to recover. I didn't go out if I could avoid it. I sat inside and cried, and cried, and asked myself how this could have happened to me. When I got tired of crying, I crocheted scarves and bed pieces for my son and grandchildren. I watched television. But mostly I just moped around my little apartment with my long face, looking pitiful. In the spring, when it began to get warm, I would look out my windows. I could hear laughter, people joking, and mothers calling to their children. Sometimes I even heard parts of a church service held in a building nearby. Life was passing me by week after week and I didn't care. Someone told me that I shouldn't look bad and feel bad at the same time. It was one or the other or neither. Somehow they got me to put on my make-up. Occasionally I would catch a glimpse of myself in the mirror and somewhere I saw a hint of a smile.

Right around the one year mark after the divorce, I woke up and realized that I had been alone all of this time. I had to make it on my own and staying cooped up in my place was no way to live. When I stepped outside into the warm sun, it was the most marvelous feeling, all over my body. The rays woke me up kind of like Big Momma's voice used to do.

Now that I knew I had to continue on my own, I had to decide what to do with the rest of my life. Fredi tried to get me to pursue a singing career. I did sing for a little while and I performed at a few hot spots, but the industry was different now and I realized that I no longer had a heart for the business, no part of it. I even thought about Black Swan. Their motto was, "The only true black recording studio." When I was a teenager and had recorded for them, it had really been something. But the place was down in the basement in a junky room full of boxes, with little equipment. There really was nothing down there. While I was certain that technology had improved in the record business, I had no interest at all in going back to it.

I began to think about different jobs and careers. Most of them were eliminated when I looked at the training required compared to what I was naturally good at and what I liked to do. I looked at the papers and read stories and eventually I realized that I, too, was human and that it might be nice to have some company or at least go out on a date.

Oh, I longed to have my Bunny Boy back, but the thought of dating was just ridiculous. It didn't terrify me, but it just didn't fit in at this point in my life. Young girls and teenagers went on dates, puppy love stuff. I was in my late thirties, twice divorced with one loving son, but I hadn't been on a date in almost twenty years. Eventually, I realized I had to try. Maybe there was another Adam out there. I went down to this heritage place. They wanted to interview and tape me at my place. I was reluctant at first, but later I agreed. The same man who interviewed me at my apartment came to school and taped me there teaching. The day he taped me at school was my birthday. He had brought all this paraphernalia, lights, and so on, so he could photograph everything. He said, "You know you are a birthday girl, where would you like dinner?" That's all he had to say. I went in and called Jean-Claude Baker and told him that I was coming down to dinner and would be bringing this man so we'd need a reservation for two at Chez Josephine's. We went to dinner and we had a good time.

This man called me during the week. He took me to see *Showboat*. I saw the role I would have played years ago. The show was fabulous. He also took me to see the Delaney Sisters. He reintroduced me to Broadway. It was a very kind gesture. But the night we went to dinner, when we got in the cab, he kept leaning over to me and I just kept moving back over in the corner away from him because I couldn't quite understand. When it did hit me, I said to myself, "He's in the wrong pew because I ain't looking for no man. And surely not him!"

I was listening to the radio and heard about a place on Broadway called Savannah Chicken, a restaurant. Well, with that name I just had to try it, so I mentioned the place to my friend. We went there and sat at the table talking. We had eaten, the food was good, then he committed his first mistake.

"I'm going to get you cable," he said.

I'm not a late nighter and I don't need all of those channels, so I didn't pay him any mind. A few days later he called me up in the morning and told me the cable man would be over the next day, Friday. I asked him at what time. He said some time between one o'clock and five o'clock. Then he added that he'd be at my place at twelve. Right away I told him that I had an appointment. He said, "No, it can't be." He asked about the appointment and I told him it was at school. I felt that he was being pushy and trying to tell me what to do. He was trying to take advantage of me. So he stopped calling me. I know what I like to do and paying a cable bill every month is not one of them. I wasn't interested in this man other than to take me to dinner and to sit down and have a nice conversation. He certainly didn't look like no Adam Powell to me.

Then there was another man by the name of Schuster, like the Schuster clucks. Well, I used to sit and ride in his truck with him. But Schuster died. And then there was a dentist up in Boston that I flirted around with for a little while, and he died. And then somebody else died. I seem to kill all the men. So I thought to myself maybe I am the widow of death, I'm going to let these men alone.

But I did continue to go on dates. The men were affluent, attractive, and well-educated, but they still didn't compare to my Bunny. They would be wonderful catches for almost any other woman but they did nothing for me. I wanted for them to remain casual acquaintances and they generally wanted more.

Not long after the three deaths, I met someone very special who thought he could change my mind about men. I decided to give this one an honest try. I started keeping company with this man who I called Papa, a doctor. He got me the cutest miniature white poodle so I wouldn't be alone. Babette was a wonderful little companion. I took her to the island in the summer and she was small enough to stay with me in my apartment in New York during the winter time.

Maybe it was Babette's perfectly groomed fur, but I had always liked fooling with hair, so I decided to go to barbering school. Mother Powell had cut her husband's hair, and I had watched, wondering if Adam would ever let me cut his. Papa paid for my schooling and got me all of my instruments and what not. The school was down on the Bowery, in the worst neighborhood. I forgot how long it took, but I got my license. They thought it was nice to have a woman around. I was the only one. I became the favorite student when I brought them my famous brownies from time to time.

The class was full of young men, mostly boys coming home from the army now that World War II was over. Two black guys were stationed near the window. One day I came to class and it was really raining hard. Across the street on the ground near a bench there was a man lying down. The rain was just pouring down on him. Just as hard as it fell, it ran off. He didn't budge. The two guys had seen the man and thought he was a drunk. This was not exactly the best neighborhood. But when I saw him, I asked Carl to call the police. It turns out the guy was dead.

With my license and some practice under my belt I was ready for clients. When people came in, they were assigned to a particular barber. This one man sat down in my chair. When I let the chair down to start on him, he asked me to sit him back up, and I did. He looked up and saw me with a razor in my hand. Then he said to Carl, "Hey man, you goin let that 'oman put that razor on me?" Carl nodded and I asked the man what was the matter.

"Hey lady, you see dis y'ere," he said, and I looked very closely, inspecting his ear.

He said, "A 'oman cut it off with a razor." Indeed the top part of his ear was gone.

I stood my ground because I knew I was a good barber. I told him, "Sir, I'm not here to cut your ears off." I was very firm. "I'm here to give you a shave and a hair cut, and a facial if you wish."

He decided to give me a try. I took my time with him and made sure everything was just so. I finally got finished with him. I sat him up and was brushing off the hair and what not. I took his apron off. He looked at himself in the mirror real good and inspected my work.

He said, "Lady, you sho did make me purdy! Now how much is that?"

In those days a haircut was about seventy-five cents and a shave was about thirty-five cents. With everything included, the whole bill came to about three dollars. He pulled out a great big wad of money, peeled off a fifty dollar bill, and said to me.

"Now you made me sa purdy, now here, this is yo tip." He tipped me fifty dollars! I couldn't believe it. It was a good day in the shop that day. I was the envy of all the other barbers.

All kinds of people would come by. Little Italian salesmen would stop by who couldn't speak a word of English. I would just do them, take care of business, and say thank you. One day I had a drunken judge come in. I was very nervous with him in the chair. I nicked him with the razor and the blood started running. Honey, I flew upstairs and Carl was right behind me.

He said, "Belle what's the matter?"

I said, "I'm going home. I don't want to be a barber. I'm going home."

"Belle, you didn't do anything. The razor cuts close. Finish the customer. Go back downstairs and finish that man," Carl insisted.

I refused, "No, I'm not! I'm going home." Carl saw that

I was far too upset to handle a customer with a sharp razor. I sat there and calmed myself down but I didn't go back. He finished the man because I was scared. That was the first time I had ever nicked anybody.

I didn't really go into barbering to pursue it as a living and work in a shop, it was just something to do for a while, to clear my head. But I tell you, I would cut anybody's hair who would let me. I used to cut my son's hair. I cut my grandson's hair and any of his acquaintances. If they let me, I'd cut their hair. I really liked it. Now I can barely grab the scissors. I remember a time when I would be sitting on the subway staring at all the men's necks. I'd say to myself, "Oh, if I just had my clippers now, I could clean his neck. His neck is dirty."

Rose Morgan had a beauty shop up on 145th Street. She gave me a chair and I stayed up there for a while. I had a picture made of me cutting hair up there. I did it for a couple of years and then I stopped to pursue other interests. I still have all of my barbering equipment. I only felt a twinge of guilt when I left my customer's for the summer to go up to the island. Papa used to come up and visit. First he would stay at Shearer Cottage. Then he started staying at the place across the street from me.

I looked forward to seeing my clients when I got back to the city, but I really began to look forward to Papa's visits. He used to come in every Wednesday from Jersey, his day off. He'd spend the day with me and we'd go to dinner. We usually went downtown, especially to seafood places. We both loved seafood. He was always up, and in a good mood. He was married at the time. They lived together, but it was in name only. I didn't think anything of it. He had a daughter but she was grown. I liked him a lot and was getting comfortable with his presence.

Not long after, I finished the barbering training, Papa proposed. He was a very nice man, but I didn't know if I could do it again, marry a third time. Papa was very sweet, but he didn't compare to Adam. I think when I was courting him, I realized that no one else would measure up to Adam. I don't know exactly where that left me. I told him I'd have to think about it. He was extremely disappointed. I was leaning toward marrying him and I think I would have, but in the end, I didn't have to make the decision. He committed suicide. I was devastated. I don't know how I fooled myself into believing that it would work out. I couldn't do to someone else what Hazel had done to me and expect that to be okay.

After leaving barbering, I knew where my heart really was and what I needed to do. I didn't even have to think about it. While at the church, I focused on the youth. When Adam was on the Council, I had focused on the youth. I should be working with young people and their education. When I decided to volunteer at one of the local schools, friends warned me that it was a bad idea, a very bad idea. I was too light to work in one of the ghetto schools. The kids might think I was white and attack me out of anger. The kids couldn't and wouldn't learn, were rebellious, bordering on hostile, and it just wasn't worth it. There were lots of other good opportunities that needed volunteers.

It turned out that the school I'd be working at was one of those schools known by a number rather than a name, and the number of my school was a well known code for special needs children. The system had given up on these kids, had decided that they were too difficult to be educated in regular schools. No one gave up on me when I was a child, and Lord I gave them a time, so I wouldn't give up on these children. They needed someone to believe in them.

I ignored the rantings and ravings of friends and went right on to school. From the very beginning, I could see that the children would be a challenge. One of the class bullies decided he wanted to make a fool of me early on so he could show the rest of the class who was in charge. He was outraged that I wanted him to do his homework and study every day. I didn't waste much time on him because I knew he was ready for an argument.

"Suit yourself, little man," I said. "It makes me no difference if you don't want to learn. I've got mine. I can read and you cannot." After a bit of jeering, a hush fell over the room. I kept right on with the lesson and within a short while Mr. Smarty Pants had joined right in to obtain the knowledge he and his classmates needed so desperately. Ignoring him so he couldn't take time away from the others worked well with this particular student. What these kids needed was some no-nonsense structure and discipline, applied in a firm but caring manner so they could see that there was a reason that they should care about themselves.

Just before the Easter holiday, I made some eggs and took them to school in a nice basket. That day we reviewed our phonics and the alphabet. I so wanted these babies to learn to enunciate and speak properly. If they didn't get it now, they would never get it, and would be doomed to repeat the bad mistakes of pronunciation for the rest of their lives.

When we finished our lesson, we dyed the eggs various colors and added further decorations. Then we settled down for a story. The eggs were different colors and the story mentioned something about color. I had the children each put his hand out and we formed a big circle. I put my hand in too. I asked the children what color was I. A bunch of little voices all said, "white."

I told them, "No!"

"I'm colored, black just like all of you," I said. I explained that there are lots of different shades of this same color. When God created black people, He created the most beautiful and diverse flower garden ever, from alabaster white to ebony black, that's how Old Man Powell put it. I told them everyone in the room was black and they should always be proud of that because that's how God made them.

Sometimes when I first went into a new classroom, I might ask the children if they had ever heard of Adam Clayton Powell, Jr. Most of them had not, because they were too young. I would take the opportunity to give them a civics lesson and explain all the good things he had done and why we should all appreciate him. Then we would find a picture of him and we would go over the complexion issue.

CHAPTER 18

The Fall of Adam

Little Preston, we called him "Tommy," and his younger sister Tia were growing like weeds. Their appetites weren't far behind their bones. As the dutiful grandmother, it was my job to spoil them worse than rotten. I was especially concerned about them now since Preston and his wife had decided to break up. My son had moved out with my grandson, Tommy, and Tia was visiting her brother and father for a few days but would return to her mother. On this particular visit we double checked the time of the flight that would take Tia back to Winston, Salem, North Carolina. I reminded myself to call Bubba when I got home from the airport. He was in St. Croix. His wife had not survived heart surgery three months earlier. He was still in mourning and not doing too well.

We couldn't believe it when we got word that Bubba had had a heart attack. He was in the hospital but was expected to recover. Shirley, his daughter, went out to be with him. When she had to return home, his other daughter, Jackie, went out to St. Croix. The doctors at the hospital encouraged us to believe that he would survive. Just as we were hoping to hear that he had fully recovered, we heard about his death.

I was in the living room at home watching television, darning Preston's sock when I heard a key in the door. I was surprised because it was the middle of the afternoon. Preston came in. He worked at the VA hospital. I thought something was wrong and looked right at him waiting for him to say something. He told me Bubba was gone and swept out of the room like he couldn't deliver the bad news. I asked him what he meant. He said, "Gone, Belle. He's dead."

I was stunned. I sat still in the chair, holding the needle and sock refusing to believe his words. As the tears started to flow, I got up and turned off the television. Without thinking, I turned on the radio, more to drown out my own sobs. Not Bubba, who chased me around every square, and grossed me out with every worm he could find, who was there for me when Adam left. Not my big brother, Bubba. The pain of losing my brother was absolutely devastating. The warm fuzzy memories from my childhood overpowered me. Bubba had died because he couldn't survive without the wife he adored. He was a real man, a true husband.

Someone on the radio said something that I recognized. I tried to pay attention for a second.

"Adam Clayton Powell Jr. is dead," the voice said. I wanted the voice to take it back. Didn't it know that my brother had just died and I couldn't handle the two of them leaving the same day within ten minutes of each other.

I know, I thought. The station must be wrong. They have made a mistake. They've made mistakes before and this must be just another one of their outlandish errors. I'll change the station. But the details of Adam's death were being reported on all of the stations.

I stumbled back to the couch. I knew Preston was upset about Bubba, but he would be devastated about Adam. Adam had been Preston's surrogate father from the time he was a young boy until he enlisted in the Navy. "Ad," Preston called him. When he came home from school, he would rush past me and ask, "Where's Ad?" Would Preston forgive Adam now, for cutting Preston off after our divorce? After teaching him how to fish, how to run the projector at the church, and introducing him to important people like Louis Armstrong. Adam taught Preston the simple things a young man needs to know about life, then Adam denied him as though Preston were a complete stranger. Preston had written him a letter asking if Tommy and Tia could come visit. They had never met or seen their grandfather. Adam said no. It was devastating.

I left Long Island early in the morning on the train and headed home. Every paper had a headline that Congressman Adam Clayton Powell Jr. had passed. I sat there on the train and looked at the headlines and tried to comprehend how two of the closest people to me in the world could leave on the same day. And they had been very close before the divorce.

Adam had been in declining health for a number of years. He had suffered heart attacks and eventually lost his battle with cancer. He had also been ill as a kid and was fortunate to survive through childhood. Bubba on the other hand was in good health. We never expected to lose him so soon. Bubba's death left a gaping hole in the family that could never be filled. While everyone was in Long Island at Bubba's house paying their respects, looking at pictures, and telling stories about our wonderful brother, someone came up with the idea of a private viewing of Adam before the funeral on Saturday.

Fredi contacted the church and requested a private viewing for me at the Duncan Funeral Home. The home indicated that it would be happy to oblige. Several hours before the agreed upon time, I called my friend Carolyn Jones who was to take me to see Adam. She noted the tone of irritation in my voice and asked what was wrong. The funeral home wanted me to come by earlier because it had received calls threatening to blow up the place if Adam's body wasn't turned over to the people of Harlem.

Carolyn came over immediately. I had already changed clothes. I wore my light gray suit with the white collar and cuffs. We drove to the funeral home in silence. At the door, wooden horses blocked our entry while two police cars sat at the curb at attention. Two black policemen stood vigilant on guard at the entrance. Pedestrians were forced to walk in the street because the sidewalk was blocked. I thought there would be large noisy crowds but there were only a few people around and they were going about their normal affairs. Of course, some of them slowed down to see what the police were doing but then they continued on their way.

The press had said there were demonstrators marching past the funeral home blocking the entryway. The owner had requested that they permit me, Adam's first wife, to have a private visit and they had agreed. One of the officers approached our car and in no uncertain terms told us that the public would be permitted to view the body the following day. My throat was frozen, but Carolyn spoke up.

"This is Mrs. Adam Clayton Powell Jr.," she said, looking him straight in the eye.

Immediately his demeanor changed. Kindly he asked the owner who was near the front door if we could come in. They let us in but appeared very nervous, no doubt concerned about the return of the unruly crowds. The funeral director greeted me warmly, had us wait briefly, went into the chapel, and came back to escort us in.

Except for Adam in the casket and a black liberation flag, the room was empty. It was a stark contrast to what I had expected. There were no flowers. The room was quiet. The owner remained at the back in front of the closed chapel door. Carolyn stayed at one of the pews in back to give me some privacy with Adam. I moved forward to the casket at a snail's pace. I didn't want to see him like this, but I had to say goodbye. At last I reached the edge of the casket and saw that face that was so striking even in death. Tomorrow, the funeral would make up for this bare room. People from all over the country and the world would attend. The media would be out in full gear. This town of Harlem would be in mourning for weeks, unable to forget the man who gave them, "Keep the faith, baby!" The police barricades would barely be able to hold back the crowds. Approximately 100,000 mourners would pay their final respects. Not even the snow and freezing weather could keep them back. The service would be attended by nearly fifteen thousand people but I would not be one of them.

I could not be part of the media frenzy and gossip, our love was too good for that. His second wife, that woman, and Yvette Diago, his estranged third wife, would attend along with his companion from Bimini. I wanted no part of it.

I had a few private words with Adam, my Bunny Boy. I couldn't stop the tears from flowing. I had only seen him twice since our divorce. In the late 1950s, Adam was speaking near the Hotel Teresa. I saw a large crowd and wondered what was going on. Then I heard his voice and I couldn't leave. When he saw me, there was a look of sheer delight on his face. The second time was at Abyssinia. We both attended the funeral of a friend. When I found him looking at me from the pulpit, he turned away like he was embarrassed.

When Daddy Pops passed away, I was actually surprised to get a letter of condolence from Adam. He knew how close I was to my father. He addressed me as Isabel. It was a very kind gesture. Even with Adam, his son-in-law, my father would walk into a room with little candies or breath mints in his pockets, and squeeze one into Adam's hand. He always told Adam to have a nice day.

I reminded Adam that we wouldn't be able to go fishing any more. I wanted to tell him about Bubba but figured he must already know. I said a prayer for his soul. He knew that I loved him like no one else could, that he had given me the best years of my life, and that all was forgiven.

Seeing him this way was a bit odd. Adam was a man of action, of fiery speeches, helping the underdog, but here he was in a near empty room with not a hint of music or noise. I left the chapel knowing that Bunny regretted what he had done and that he had always loved me. Carolyn came up to view the body for a few minutes and then she left the chapel. She was waiting for me in the reception area when I finished. "I've seen him," is all I could say to her. When the car pulled away from the funeral home, I was still crying.

For years after we were divorced I'd be sitting in the Bunny Cottage in the living room or doing something in the kitchen, and I could almost hear him walking on the floors upstairs. He was tall and weighed over two hundred pounds. It sounded almost like he was jumping on the floor boards. I would turn my head, expecting to see him coming down the stairs, but he was never there. He had selected most of my clothes. I couldn't help but wonder what he would think of me now that I wore pants, a fairly recent development. It was always important to Adam to go out looking good. He never so much as wore blue jeans or even khakis.

It was really hard to forgive Adam for denying me the opportunity to go to the White House when he was elected to Congress, but he was gone now and I *had* to forgive him. By then, he had already caught the disease of power and it would ultimately be his downfall. It's what I had prayed he would be strong enough to resist. I thought he couldn't be a good politician because he was already a preacher. But he used the church as his base support and expanded outward from there until it got so big that even he couldn't manage it. When Adam took over the church even the babies in my Tiny Tots Choir believed in his dream. He would make America a better place for them, for their future. The world would be a better place because he had been here. Hundreds of members would volunteer to be on his campaign, and work countless hours, just so he could shake their hands in person and say thank you. It was like being acknowledged by a movie star. Some of them got to take pictures with him that they would treasure for years.

While Adam was sharpening his political skills, I went from school to school in black parts of the city, to teach phonics to young kids who were poor but still deserved a chance, to work with challenged kids who the system had given up on, or to read to the children to open up their imaginations. With only one other Negro in Congress, Adam's group of "constituents" swelled to include virtually every other colored person in the country and then some. He fought a battle big enough for fifty men, too big for any one person, and yet it was a war that had to be fought.

The frequent headlines in the paper began to worry me. He achieved many victories, proposing needed legislation in a country that claimed all of its citizens were free. He also made enemies who were in high places and who could do him serious harm. Like my grandfather, I cut out articles from the paper, but my obsession was not a ship, it was Adam's political career.

I saw comments in the paper from Hazel about how wonderful her marriage was. They disturbed me at first. She sounded a bit like me, praising her perfect husband who could do no wrong. I knew she would change her tune, it was just a matter of time. I was Adam's only true love, the one he had given it all up for. Power and politics was his other love, an obsession so strong that no woman, no human could compete with.

When Adam first went to Congress, Washington, D.C. remained segregated. "Look out!" was all I could say, knowing how Adam felt about segregation and remembering our train trips. In the land of the free and the home of the brave, a growing portion of the nation couldn't go to movie theaters, eat at certain restaurants, shop at particular stores, or even go to certain hospitals where the best care was provided. Adam hated segregation. He fought it in Congress, in the District of Columbia, and all over the world with all his might.

Adam touched the hearts of people of color around the world at the Bandung Conference in Indonesia held in 1955. He had to pay to go himself because the United States boycotted the event. But as he fell deeper and deeper into politics his priorities changed. With me he had been a husband first, a preacher second, and a politician third. As his affair with his new love deepened, these priorities were completely reversed.

As he became more politician than anything else, it was the church that suffered. Sometimes he was away for months on various trips, and then there were allegations of tax evasion against the church and later against he and his wife. By the time Ester James, who Adam accused of being involved in the numbers games in Harlem, sued him for defamation, Adam acted as though he were invincible. She won an award which he refused to pay. He could have been arrested on sight. He thought about retiring but thought better of it, because he needed the political arena in order to breathe, and the Harlem community, including Abyssinia, needed him to survive.

Shortly after Lyndon Johnson took over, after the assassination of President Kennedy, the Civil Rights Act of 1964 was signed into law. Adam was very proud of his work. More or less he had touched nearly everyone in the country. He had fought for a minimum wage, for student loans, and for immigrant rights. But when poor Adam was stripped of his Committee Chairmanship in Congress after years of building up his seniority, it was more than he could take. He was accustomed to taking things away from other people, not the other way around.

As his colleagues and others here in Harlem began to attack Adam, I actually felt sorry for him. He was not perfect and may have committed some of the wrongs he was accused of. I do not condone such actions. But I knew in my heart that the attacks weren't really because of anything he had done. He took no liberties that any other Congressman had not already taken. The attacks were because he was an outspoken black man who would not shut up until the cause he was fighting for had been achieved. Most of his Congressional colleagues had done no less than Adam, yet they were willing to stand on a soapbox and point the finger at him. They wanted to tell him that he could not get away with what they could.

Each time Adam ran again for his seat in Congress, I voted for him. I thought he had the best interests of the community at heart and he knew the community better than anyone else. I was not going to let Congress dictate to me who I could have to represent me. Colored people have already been dictated to and told what to do for too much of our history in this country. Adam's hands were tied when he got his seat back because Congress took away his seniority and he couldn't propose all the legislation he had before. They had taken away his power. He lived to make life better for any group who suffered. He couldn't do it without the power, the seniority.

Eventually and sadly, I saw the community changing, with increasing crime, babies who couldn't speak proper English, young people cursing in the street, and young men wearing their pants so low you could see their drawers. A crack addict even came into my apartment and stole my wallet. These issues needed to be addressed.

Even when Charles Rangel was elected to the 92nd Congress in 1970, and ended Adam's long kingship in Harlem, what my Bunny did for this place and for this country remains a symbol of hope to all. It shows that one person *can* make a difference, that he loved Harlem, and should be remembered as a man of the people. No one had to tell me that he was broken-hearted. I could feel it in my spirit. Now that his seat was gone, he went back to his church. He had been away so often, the membership had fallen, and the deacons wanted to appoint a successor. Bunny wanted to just pick up where he left off, but he knew he had neither the energy nor the support. The cancer kept him in a great deal of pain. In a few short weeks, it took him away from me forever.

Back at my school, P.S. 56, a teacher suggested a memorial service for Adam. I would never have brought up the idea myself, but I agreed with her. I just didn't want to be made uncomfortable by having to go on stage. I wanted to remain with my class in our usual spot at the back of the auditorium. They assured me that I would be spared the embarrassment of the stage. The students knew me as Mrs. Powell but the teachers knew about Adam. I offered to supply information for the assembly. I should have known better.

At the beginning of the assembly, the principal asked the "widow and first wife of the man whose memory we are honoring today, our own, Mrs. Isabel Powell," to come up to the stage.

I was annoyed by what they had done. However, as I got nearer to the front and heard the applause, I felt appreciation. I kept my words brief. "I asked them not to do this to me. Anyhow, thank you! All of you. I've really nothing to say but that I'm here at this school because I love you." The applause was warm as I went back to my seat.

With the ceremony over, I supervised the clean up. A small group of kids who couldn't stand still for a moment gathered papers and sheets that had been left behind. One child was a bit off to himself. A little smaller than the rest, he had a look of great curiosity on his little face. He looked over at me and I smiled. He came directly over.

He turned his head to one side, stared up into my eyes and demanded, "Miz. Powell, is you a imposter?"

"A what?" I responded.

"A imposter," he repeated boldly.

I looked over at Principal Cox and nodded for him to come over so I could get the full understanding of this child's question. When he came he explained that the child had learned a new word. "But why did you ask me that?" I asked those little brown eyes.

He spoke very slowly and with care to make sure he was clearly understood.

"Is it really true that you was married to him up there?" he said looking up at Adam's huge poster.

"Yes," I told him with a smile.

He pounced his next question with suspicion, "Then what you doing down here with me?" he demanded again. I took a deep breath.

"Do you remember what I said when I was up on that platform?" I asked him. "I am here because I love you," I continued touching his face. "I meant you too."

His entire face broke out into a smile. He looked up at the oversized poster of Adam and told him, "You hear that, up there. She says she loves me down here!"

CHAPTER 19

Sisterless

In the traditional South, "Sister" is what you call the oldest girl, and "Bubba" is what you call the oldest boy. Fredi was the oldest girl in our family. We called her Sister. She had been the best Christmas gift our family had ever received. On June 28, 1994, Alzheimer's took Fredi away forever. She would have been ninety on her birthday in December. Since Little Momma passed away, Sister had always been there for me. I know we all have our appointed time to go, but in some odd way I thought she'd always be there for me. Without Fredi I felt lost and very alone.

There are so many things she did for me. When Little Momma left us, she just stepped right in and took over, refusing to let her two little sisters miss out on anything. When Adam left me, she was right there fighting him tooth and nail, the same way she defended us from anyone in the neighborhood back in Savannah. The first summer I went up to the island after our divorce, I went to see Big Momma and then straight to the train. Years ago the train used to come up and back right up to the boat. When I reached the house, I saw that Preston and Fredi had been there already. They had opened up the house and on the kitchen walls there were beautiful placards with little poems on them. One was about wealth, another was about love, and the last addressed another topic. Each was nicely framed hugging the kitchen wall near the pantry. They were the perfect thing to lift my spirits. I've kept them right there.

In 1926, Fredi starred in *Black Boy* with Paul Robeson, the most incredible actor of the day. After the show closed, Fredi couldn't find work. She decided to form a dance team with Al Moiret and give Europe a try. Fredi and Moiret toured various capitals all over Europe and were a big hit. She toured in Paris, Berlin, and London among other places. She even taught the Prince of Wales to do the Black Bottom. They stayed over in Europe for two whole years. It was while they were there that we heard the rumor that Sister had died.

Fredi was so independent. She didn't tell any of us that she was headed overseas. When we saw a huge wardrobe truck backing up to our place, we knew something was going on so she finally had to explain. That's how we found out she would be going away to Europe. She did so many things that I didn't have the courage to do. She learned how to drive and drove all the way from the east coast to the west coast in her little yellow V.W. bug when she was working on a project in Hollywood. I never learned to drive and still don't know how to swim.

Now that she's really gone, I can smile at the earlier reports of her demise. We hadn't heard from her in a long time and were beginning to get worried. The papers actually reported that she had died. It was just awful. We were so upset and we didn't know what to think. The details were kind of sketchy. Then one evening I was having dinner at *Mexico's*, one of the places where show people hang out, and in walked Fredi. She looked beautiful to me and very much alive. I screamed her name and knocked over my chair because I jumped up so fast. Her top was trimmed in fur and she looked exquisite, like an angel.

Fredi's dance act got to tour with both Eubie Blake and Duke Ellington for a while. She was thrilled to be home, doing her stuff right here. Then her partner injured himself, leaving them both unemployed. Fortunately in 1930 another colored musical came along. She was featured in *Hot Chocolates* and remained gainfully employed for a while.

When we were still young and crazy, we were actually in a play together, the two of us and Maude. *Singin the Blues* ran in late 1929 into part of 1930 at the Majestic Theater. Initially the producers sought Fredi for the part I played, but it was a singing role and Fredi didn't sing. She mentioned that she had a sister who would be perfect for the part. It worked out well for everyone. The reviews were great and the cast was called "exceptional." Fredi played the vamp which was typical for her. The three of us had a ball. Even the New York City Mayor, Jimmy Walker, presented us with flowers, kissed us on the cheek, and told us how much he had enjoyed the performance.

Fredi did so many plays and several movies. But she is probably best known for her role as Peola in *Imitation of Life*, the first movie of its kind. That movie really made people think about the issue of "passing." The original version in 1934 with Fredi, Claudette Colbert, and Louise Beavers was so good that there was no reason to do a remake. Even now the original is a real tear-jerker. Fredi was so convincing in her role that people thought she really wanted to be white. Fredi and the movie became associated with the problem of passing. She had to do interviews and talks and explain to people that she was a dramatic actress and it was her job to convince people that she was actually her character. Some people even started questioning the blackness of our family and calling the girls "Peola" in the derogatory sense of wanting to be white. Anyone who knew our family knew that we were colored through and through, no matter how light our skin was.

The summer after the movie came out I was up in Martha's Vineyard near Shearer Cottage. There were three Native American men sitting down and they had been drinking. When they saw me, they started laughing and said, "Don't worry Peola, we won't hurt you." A new word had come out of the movie. They thought this comment was very funny, but I was offended. Ironically, we weren't criticized by white people but by our own for the most part. That's one of the things that broke Sister's heart.

Fredi was a victim of her own success. After *Imitation of Life*, as usual there were so few dramatic roles for colored women, especially for women who had as much talent as Sister. She couldn't play a colored woman because she was too light. People might mistake her for white. In a couple of roles we both played we had to be what they called "dipped" to make us appear darker skinned so the audience wouldn't be offended. On the other hand, Fredi, couldn't play a white woman because of racism and segregation. These old movies were in black and white. We didn't have the technology back then that we have today, but even if movies had been in color, people still would have wondered about Sister's racial background.

After the success of *Imitation of Life*, the next project would naturally involve some type of romantic relationship. To film goers she might appear to be white, but the United States was not ready to see any kind of hugging or kissing of that type on the big screen yet. The screen was just as segregated as the country, if not more so. Fredi wanted to be an actress, not a "black" actress or a "white" actress. The stereotypes were derogatory and insulting. Colored people were so much more than mammie maids and Amos and Andy types. Back in those days, the stage was still considered the pinnacle of where only the best went. Broadway was everyone's goal. So when Sister got her Hollywood contracts and, they told her they would teach her how to act, she turned up her nose and told them they could teach her how to do movies but she already knew how to act because she had been on Broadway. My Sister, she was so bold.

In all of her movies, Sister fought to have us portrayed decently. The movies were written by white writers who used black stereotypes to make whites feel good and keep blacks in their place. Or the writers used what little knowledge they had about us to represent our entire character. In *Imitation of Life*, the writers wanted to have Sister's character say something like, "If only I were white." Sister insisted that that line be taken out. She tried to explain to the writers that what all colored people wanted was a decent life and not to be white. Anything she thought was offensive she would fight to have it deleted. In another movie, *One Mile From Heaven*, released in 1937, Sister insisted that she not appear in a servant role even though she took care of a white child. Some of her movies couldn't play in parts of the South because the Negro was out of his place and they would not have that down South.

Several other movies were made about "passing," but Fredi wasn't called for any of those films. In many movies from that time period, colored people were portrayed by whites. One explanation that Fredi received was that there weren't any competent colored actors who could do the job. That excuse just made her so mad. When Imitation of Life was redone, the part played by Fredi was given to a white actress. Lena Horne went for the role but for whatever reason it was given to the other actress.

Fredi was so disgusted by how colored entertainers were treated that she founded the Negro Actor's Guild in 1937 to unite people in their fight to be treated like human beings, the same as white people. She served as the Executive Secretary for a number of years. Time after time when plays went on the road, there would be problems with places to stay and restaurants and what have you. And even though New York was "progressive" for the day, there were some establishments that still wanted Negro entertainers to come in through the back door. They might let people like Fredi or me slip by, but darker-skinned people would have to go round the back. Fredi fought against all of that. She felt that no Negro was really free to step through the front door until all colored people, regardless of complexion, were free to walk in the front door.

When she couldn't find work in the film industry, she'd go back to the stage, to places like Club Alabam. Given her struggle with finding substantial work, her constant fight for decent roles for black people, her activism on the road when hotels and other places wouldn't let blacks in, and then her own people criticizing her like she was a traitor, well she had had enough.

She married Lawrence Brown the same year I married

Adam, but Duke Ellington had been her only true love. When she and Lawrence got divorced in 1951, she came to live in this same building with me. Kind of like Preston Sr., Lawrence had wanted her to give up her craft and wasn't crazy about so many men ogling his wife. Even though she could afford it, she really didn't want to live anywhere else. It wasn't just to be near me. When she watched new buildings go up, Fredi would comment, "They don't build them like they used to anymore. They build them out of chicken wire, match stems, and spit!" When she married her second husband, Dr. Anthony Bell, a dentist, they lived in Connecticut and he took real good care of Fredi, but left her a widow.

Fredi and I used to have such fun sometimes reminiscing about the good old days. Neither one of us could believe the lives we had lived. If only Little Momma had been around to see how big and famous her little girls had gotten. Fredi and I both knew Bill Robinson, "Bojangles." Adam and I had gone out west to visit Fredi and Bojangles when she was making the film, *One Mile From Heaven*. What a fabulous dancer he was! That man could dance as well in his sixties as he could at twenty-five. A theater named for him opened up in the city of Richmond, Virginia. Fredi and I both went down for the opening. It was one of the last events we went to before she got really sick. Talk about some fabulous clothes. A coat that she wore was a hand-painted evening coat that came from Japan. The coat was just gorgeous. I inherited it, and like a fool gave it away.

Fredi was a little like Adam in that she had always had a way with people and managed to meet the top people wherever she was involved. She had one of the best agents around and introduced other up and coming people to him who wanted a chance. When Fredi was in the home before she died, we tried to get Lena Horne to visit her. We thought it might jog her memory and help her recognize things. I told Lena that Fredi was in the nursing home and what a lovely thing it would be if Lena went up there to see her. She never did. I know what it would have meant to her in her condition to see anybody she knew from those days. She already had the love and affection of all the staff at the home. We took affront because Fredi had introduced Lena to her booking agent who was the biggest agent at the time. Lena took it on her own from there but without that first introduction, who knows?

When Fredi was still writing in her column for *The People's Voice*, one of the readers wrote in and argued that Lena Horne was underpaid for the film *Stormy Weather* and that she made far less money than Hazel Scott who she had appeared in the film with her. Fredi defended Hazel, commenting that she had paid her dues over a number of years and that's how the industry was. Lena was a relative newcomer, but once she paid her dues, she too would make the big bucks. I think Fredi might have had something a little different to say about Hazel after my divorce.

Fredi grew to despise anything that was related to movies and the theater because of what the industry had done to her. I was fortunate enough to leave show biz on a high on my own terms. I had been a star on Broadway when I left, with a bright future. Fredi's exit was less celebrated but her career much longer and full of brilliant work. But never one to give up, in the end she was able to work as a movie consultant on several films to help Hollywood try to get it right. Today colored actors and actresses have a lot more opportunity, but Fredi would say there's still not nearly enough.

One of the things that frustrated Fredi was that Hollywood thought it knew everything about colored people and didn't hesitate to portray us in any slothful way that it wanted. There was little attempt to balance good and bad qualities. After seeing many such movies filmgoers might have a distorted view of what colored people are really like. In the movies we were frequently portrayed as being loose, no good, and trifling. On the other hand, whites thought we didn't understand anything about them. They could play us but we couldn't play them. Fredi did as much as she could. When Governor Brown of California read an article about how poorly black actors were treated, he invited a number of entertainers to a special event. Fredi was to receive an award, but she refused to go. She sent back the ticket and everything. They mailed the award to her and I have it now. But that's how frustrated she had become.

The one area where I'm glad I didn't really follow Sister is with her cigarettes. She started smoking when she was barely a teenager. And she really smoked a lot. It was considered a glamorous thing back then. Smoke coming out of your nose made you look cool and sophisticated. And for entertainers like Fredi, it helped to keep your weight down.

We didn't have all the warnings from the tobacco companies like we do now, but they knew what they were doing. Tobacco is like any other narcotic except it is legal. Both Fredi and Adam were hooked. Fredi paid a terrible price for all those years of tobacco glamour when part of her lungs were removed. She never could quite get enough air after that. She really had to take it easy. If there's one thing I could tell the young people it would be for them not to smoke, ever!

I visited Sister in the home about every two weeks. There were always lots of letters from college students and actors and what have you. So I asked her if she had replied to any of them. She said no. "If I responded to everyone who writes me I'd need a secretary." I knew what she meant. The letters related to show business and she didn't want to have anything to do with that world. She had left it behind and didn't want to look back.

Fredi had appeared in a production of Run Lil' Chillun in 1933. The play was a smash hit. The remake done several years later didn't go over quite so well. One commentator wrote to *The People's Voice* and said the problem with the play was that, "It didn't run, but crawled." After Fredi stopped laughing, she responded, commenting that the play was indeed different from the earlier production but she still encouraged the actors of the new cast who had performed. She tried to stay neutral on that one, but on several other matters she let the readers speak for themselves. Fredi stayed at the paper until about 1947. Things became more tense given what Adam had done and our divorce.

One week her column was devoted to servicemen. Some of them asked for more pinup posters of Lena Horne and Hazel Scott. Another overseas military man expressed his gratitude for the publication of the paper because there wasn't a lot to read where he was in Europe. Another colored fellow who was serving in Hawaii remarked that he didn't experience the racism and prejudice that was customary in much of the South. He said he was having a great time. To demonstrate his point, he sent a picture of himself with a lovely hula girl, both grinning.

Fredi cared so much about our military and our colored men in general. She was definitely a civil rights activist but she was also a patriot at heart. Whether it was men in the military or the boys right here at home, Fredi gave them her love and support and fought for what was right. She worked with the NAACP and supported anti-lynching legislation. She marched and picketed and fought like hell for civil rights not because she wanted a hand out, but because she believed in a fair chance, and she gave the police in Harlem hell. They were going around beating on colored men with their billy clubs. She wrote letters, put comments in her column, and spoke to the contacts that she had in the city to address this ugly matter. Fredi was a tiger who never quit.

Sister was one of the most beautiful and talented women in the world. Sadky, she did not have any children. Back then babies and show business didn't mix very well. If people did have children they were more likely to get out of the business. But back in the roaring twenties, quitting the business was the very last thing on anybody's mind. Also Fredi raised us, we were her kids. She knew what hell it was to raise a family and maybe she chose not to go through that again!

CHAPTER 20

Me and My Boyfriend

      I thought I had been through everything life could throw at me. Then the doctor came in and knocked the wind out of me. The diagnosis was cancer. I was only in my sixties, too young to die. When she started talking about good news I just stared at her. How could there be any good news to a thing like cancer. She was going to do further tests. The "good news" was that they had found it early and I would have a very high chance of making a full recovery.

      Cancer! I had never thought about it, but maybe that's what took Little Momma away. Medical science barely had any treatments at all for it back then. Now there were all kinds of walks, runs, and fundraisers to help. My body wouldn't let me do the walks or runs but I did give to the fundraisers. I had helped them and now they would help me.

      I had to be strong, like Big Momma. When I wanted to cry and just give up after so many personal battles in my life, I held on and thought about that woman and her fierce determination. Big Momma was operated on for cancer of the breast. The doctor told her she couldn't eat certain types of food. She looked at the doctor and told him, "God grewed it and I'm gonna eat it!"

      My lump was in my right breast. I didn't need chemotherapy but I would require a lumpectomy. I had to learn an entirely new vocabulary just to try to understand what the doctors were saying. So far there's been no return, thank God, and I only have to take one pill for it every morning. They got it all out and I healed up without any problems. I consider myself blessed. I knew I would be okay when I stopped thinking about me and started thinking about Big Momma. If she survived it, I could survive it. I was her granddaughter.

Shortly after the cancer, I had spinal surgery. They found out that I had spurs going into my spine that were pressing on it. After the surgery, I began to walk with a cane. It's nice and sturdy, it's here all the time whether I need it or not, and it helps me walk, so I call it my boyfriend.

Back in the twenties when I was doing all kinds of moves on the dance floor, I would never have imagined that I'd be walking with a cane, have arthritis, and suffer from sciatica. I was fortunate enough to star in three Broadway plays, do a few movie shorts, and perform in a number of other arenas before I left the movies for matrimony. In *Bomboola* my costume had a tail. My hair was fixed in a wild style to resemble fur, and I performed a wicked dance that would just knock your socks off. I did several plays off Broadway and even spent a short while on radio.

One of the most memorable things I did was a film short called *St. Louis Blues*. Bessie Smith made the song by the same title into a great hit with her powerful voice. It also featured Louis Armstrong which guaranteed that it would be popular. This was in 1925. A few years later, the writers, Kenneth Adams and W.C. Handy, thought it would make a good movie short. They were right. Film shorts were played before main features like cartoons used to be. In the movie, Jimmy Mordecai, Bessie's no good boyfriend, was cheating on her with me. We actually had a fight on screen where she beats me up with a pillow. The movie was done in 1929. It was Bessie's only film appearance. She had an untimely death after an auto accident in 1937. They couldn't get her to the hospital in time. She had had a rough life, but she was nice to me.

Unlike Bessie Smith, Ethel Waters was a real meanie, I mean bitter, a witch. I don't know if she liked anybody, but she sure didn't like me and Fredi. One time Fredi got real sick. She had to take this medication and she just wasn't able to function. I had gone to rehearsal with Fredi and was pretty comfortable with her part. The director asked me to step in for my sister. Ethel nearly had a fit. It's one thing to show surprise but she was contorting her face and rolling her eyes. As every entertainer knows, the show must go on. Even when Fredi came back to the show, Ethel had a real bad attitude. She didn't like my best friend Maude Russell either.

Maude had a beautiful voice and took every opportunity she could to showcase it. Once, she sang with Fats Waller's band. Ethel wouldn't even come to the show, she sent her maid. The maid returned and told Ethel that Maude was over there knocking 'em dead.

Maude had been the understudy for Ethel Waters for a year and nine months and never once got to go on stage. Ethel didn't want to share the limelight with anyone. Maude was working with a Mr. Berlin, one of the men who wrote the show, and he said to her, "Russell, won't you trip her," referring to Ethel Waters. That's how well people thought of Ethel Waters.

Another time, Adam and I had gone down to see her in a cabaret on Broadway. We sent word that we were there and would like to see her backstage. She made us wait for two hours and then had someone tell us she couldn't see us. She really didn't care about people. She was mean-spirited. Most show business people had a little bit of grace and decorum about them. She had none.

Josephine Baker, now, she was a gracious lady. People always ask if I danced with Josephine Baker. The answer is no, but Fredi, my sister, and Maude, my best friend, knew Baker pretty well. They danced with her in Paris and traveled around with her when plays were on tour.

I did have the pleasure of seeing Josephine Baker perform once. I saw Baker the last time she came to America. By then I was working in the school system. A girlfriend of mine who was a teacher bought the tickets and we got seats right up front. We were so excited. I sent a note backstage with one of the usherettes who had seated us and told Baker that I was the sister of Fredi Washington and the daughter-in-law of Mother Powell, who had met Baker in Europe. I asked her if I could come backstage after the show to see her. The people were crazy for Baker and the crowd was very thick. It would be impossible to get to see her.

The show was one of the most incredible I have ever seen in my life. It was two solid hours of constant entertainment. In one scene she came out on a motorcycle that was as long as the entire stage. She was dressed in a sexy tight black leather outfit. All of her costumes were fantastic. She continued to perform but now she knew who I was. I had also mentioned in my note where I was sitting in the audience. During a certain act, she came down off the stage with little bottles of perfume. She walked up and down the aisle just once and threw these little bottles to a few people. I got one of the bottles.

After the show I found the usherette who was going to bring me to Josephine Baker's room. With my hand in hers, I left my friend in her seat. The usherette pulled me through the crowd which was no small feat. Everyone was clamoring to get to Baker. I will never as long as I live forget her and what I saw. She greeted me warmly. She had very heavy bags under her eyes, kind of like the Duke. From the audience you couldn't tell because there were little tiny sequins under her eyes but I got a close up view. She didn't spend much time with me. I didn't expect her to. She was weary.

At this time the woman was about seventy-six years old, and she had been on that stage for two hours except for quick costume changes. Her costumes were absolutely stunning.

When I had written Baker the note to go backstage, I told her that I was the daughter-in-law of Mother Powell. Adam's mother may have been older, but she got around in her day and knew so many people. She was a personal friend of Mrs. Henson, Matthew Henson's wife. Adam had been trying to get him up to the island forever but never could. Then Mother Powell and Adam got him to come. I was thrilled. He was very quiet but very charming. We were showing him around the island and I had admired a really nice plant hanger in a store. When Mr. Henson came back by that evening he presented the plant hanger to me as a gift. We hung it up immediately and plants seem to thrive when they are hung in that special spot.

Louis Armstrong was a favorite visitor. He had just come back from Japan and we invited him up to the island. He stopped by and we had a good old roaring time. Hycie Curtis, Armstrong, and myself had taken a drawing picture together. He gave it to Hycie to give to me and I colored it in and placed it on the wall for all to see.

At a party on the island, I had the opportunity to meet Betty Shabazz. Once we started talking, we couldn't stop. We exchanged addresses, were intent on going to dinner and a play in New York, but before we had a chance to get together, she passed away.

When Adam and I were married, so many celebrities and big names would come through the house on a regular basis over a period of nearly twelve years. I cannot remember them all. Joe Louis was a fairly frequent visitor and Mrs. Roosevelt came over for dinner once. She was charming. However, after the divorce, I was no longer part of the elite and, with few exceptions, the people who used to call on me and Adam didn't call on me by myself. Now he had become a Congressman and even more people were calling on him.

When he first started out, it was Harlem that attracted Adam. It was vibrant, and needy, but people had hope. Adam gave them even more. The city has changed so much, sometimes I can barely recognize it. I stick to the old values of how I was raised. We never went home to Mother without calling first. People in New York drop by people's houses for something to do. Nobody drops by on me. They just don't do it. It was a thing that was established when Adam and I were married and continues to this day. Arrangements were made. We certainly had plenty of company. We'd take all the people from the church and we'd go fishing on the boat and what not. But I think its bad manners to just drop in on anyone. You don't know what they're doing. My sister, Fredi, lived on the other side of my apartment building. I never, ever went over there without calling first. Not that she didn't want to see me, but she might have been busy.

I'm a very private person. Nobody comes to my house on Martha's Vineyard if they aren't invited. Don't come by and ding dong on my bell and ask me to put you up for the night. No way. Take yourself down to the beach and lay it down on the sand. None of my friends from the good old days would have thought of just dropping in. It would have been considered rude. Most of them are gone, so it's up to me to let my new friends know what the rules are. I do miss the old folks a lot, but I will always have my boyfriend, he follows the rules.

Maude and I had to follow the rules. We were both getting so old that we really couldn't get around by ourselves. We talked on the phone several times a week. I never hung up from talking with Maude without a smile on my face. She called me one day and said she had had a dream about Adam. Adam and I were at the water's edge and Adam said we were going to go out there on the waves. Before she could even get real good into the dream I stopped her. I said Maude, "Listen, don't come telling me nothing about Adam or Hazel. They're over there and let them stay there. They're gone and I'm here and I'm too busy trying to live." She just laughed.

Maude was not my blood sister but, when she died, I felt like I had lost a sister. We had been friends for well over fifty years. Maude had been a dancer, performed on and off Broadway, toured overseas, and could sing her behind off. They called her the "Slim Princess." She was a rare person, so kind and sweet. She outlived five husbands and waited until she was 104 before she died. Years ago at one of our family gatherings, Bubba made a big banner and welcomed her into the Washington family. After that we started calling her Sister too. When Fredi first got to New York, she didn't know how to put on her make-up properly. Maude took her aside and showed her. They had been friends since then.

When I started going up to the house on the island to open it up, or if I had to travel somewhere, Adam would send Maude with me. She was a little more sophisticated and had done lots of plays on the road. She definitely more worldly and knew her way around in places where I had never been. She was really something.

Maude had known that Adam was fooling with Hazel for maybe a year before the news came out. She didn't tell me because she was my friend and she didn't want me to be hurt or to ruin our friendship. And Adam could be very vindictive to people who pried into his business. She just wanted to stay out of it. Wingie, our chauffeur, told her every move that Adam made. He knew Maude would not open her mouth to anyone. Adam had promised Wingie that he would get him a prosthetic arm and a job with the federal government, but somehow when Adam left me, he forgot about those promises. I felt so bad for Wingie.

After Maude passed away, there was hardly anyone left from the old days. One of the few old timers to hang on was a close friend of the family, Bobby Short. We would go down to the Carlyle Hotel where he worked all the time. He had a wonderful charming voice. When he was done with a set or during his break he would come over to our table and sit down and talk with us. He was always warm and very funny. He was perpetually in a good mood and always smiling. Each year he brought his sunny disposition with him from the south of France where he spent his summers.

He absolutely adored Fredi. He worshiped the ground she walked on. The relationship was purely platonic because he was gay. She had taken him around and introduced him to everybody when he first came to Harlem. He really appreciated that, and then our family kind of took him in. When I heard about his recent death in 2005, it really broke my heart. Just a few weeks before he passed away, he had sent me a bunch of mugs with a drawing of him on the side posing with a little Dalmatian. It was the cutest thing. I will treasure it all the more now that he has gone. Oh, will he be missed.

Several years before, Bobby had come to my ninetieth birthday party wearing his tux. About sixty of my closest friends came to Chez Josephine's in Manhattan to celebrate the occasion. Jean-Claude's place is wonderful. The affair was fabulous. Evelyn Horad, a close friend, suggested that Bobby Short sing for us. In typical Bobby Short fashion, he offered to sing if I would dance. Of course, I couldn't. I was there with my wooden boyfriend, but my back stopped cooperating in dancing a long time ago.

During the speeches at the party, another close friend, Roslyn, said no matter what time of day she calls me, I jump into positive. My wonderful son, Preston, praised me as he should. Then someone referred to me as a Renaissance woman. And our dearest friend Bobby Short talked about meeting Fredi and I back in 1945 when he came to New York to become a star.

The cake was covered with ninety candles. They were the trick candles that kept relighting. When Tommie blew them out, I wished I could dance the way I used to. Bobby did favor us with a song. Then a wonderful musical historian, Elliot Hurwitt, surprised us all with the recordings of the songs I did with Black

Swan. Finally, we saw all the old pictures from back in the day. We laughed so hard, we started coughing. It was really a great time. The party reminded me that I have had a great life and if I had to do all over again there are very few things that I would change.

Years before, Jackie Onassis had approached me about writing a "tell all" book about Adam. She seemed disappointed when I declined. Like her, I had been married to one of the greatest men of his generation to walk this earth. She hadn't written a "tell all" book about Kennedy. She should expect no less of me. I would not tarnish Adam's memory. But maybe a book was not a bad idea, one written from my perspective … Who else would tell the story?

CHAPTER 21

The Dream

I had a dream about Adam. He was knocking on my apartment door. When I answered the door he waved for me to come on. Wherever my Bunny is, I don't want him rushing me. I am too busy trying to live and spread a little joy around. I'm going to be dead for a long time so I would like to enjoy every living moment I have left. That's one of the reasons I decided that it was okay to use his name. For over twenty years I refused to use his name for anything. Then I realized that I was his wife too and I had a right to use the name because it was my name too. Now if I have a problem and I mention the name, somehow the problem gets resolved very quickly. It's a delight. I am going to celebrate me now, for however long I have left here.

When Adam and I divorced and I got the Bunny Cottage, I never imagined that Adam would not return to Martha's Vineyard, a place where he had spent every free moment he had and that he loved so much. The Cottage is as much a part of him as it is of me. There are so many memories and laughs hidden between the Cottage and the shore. Even though I have a little more solitude in Oak Bluffs than in New York, I do believe that one day the island will just split wide open and we'll sink into the sea. It has become a very popular vacation destination, lots of millionaires are building homes on the island, and there are just too many cars and people. Now you have to make reservations well ahead of time to come over on the ferry.

At this point in my life, I prefer the relative calm and peace up at the island to the hustle and bustle of New York City. The stairs at the Cottage annoy me but somehow I manage with the help of my boyfriend. Harlem has changed so much. It's difficult to get around and the young people seem to have little respect for their elders even when they walk on canes, but Harlem will always be a special place to me. I lived a dream life in these streets and no one can take that away from me. When the fairytale turned into a nightmare, I thought I would never survive. But glory to God, I'm still here. After all this time, the wounds are certainly healed.

One of the sweetest pleasures is to live long enough to actually see that what goes around comes around. But I'll get to that later. I thought I would never get over Adam, but at least I've learned to live without him. I'm proud of myself because I've managed to meet one of Adam's other wives. I don't have to worry about Hazel because she is already gone. I met Yvette, Adam's third wife, when Mayor Dinkins was going to Africa. It was summertime. I was invited to an affair for Dinkins on Central Park West. Adam IV came. I was sitting down in his seat and there was this lady there who didn't know if we had met. I had already met Adam, the son, at the Schomburg when they showed a movie about Adam taken in Bimini. We became good friends. They brought his entourage over to meet me but I explained that I already knew him.

He stepped up with a big grin on his face and said in his cute little accent, "Mrs. Powell, I want you to meet my mother Mrs. Powell." And he introduced me to his mother, a heavy set Puerto Rican woman. Then he introduced me to his aunt. And there was a third person, a lovely young beautiful brown-skinned girl who he never did introduce. Not be left out, she moved forward saying, "And Mrs. Powell, I am Mrs. Powell, the fourth." I shook her hand and smiled.

New York News was there. I was interviewed by an African young man from Columbia University. Then they lined us up to take a picture. They put Adam by me and it was so funny. He's just as tall as his father was and looks just like him. He looked down and said, "But this Mrs. Powell is not my mother. That Mrs. Powell is my mother." So they moved him down and put him next to his mother and they took the picture.

I showed Adam IV a picture of a pair of his father's shoes. He had become interested in local politics and planned to run for office. I told him, "If you can't fit his shoes you stretch your feet to fit them." He knew what I meant, that despite what had happened between me and his father, his father was a great man who did great things for his people and for all oppressed people everywhere.

Adam would be proud of his son, Adam IV. I didn't even know that he was running for office when I invited two friends over to dinner. We were talking about his primary campaign. One of the women was certain that he had lost and the other was uncertain but thought that he had won. He called me the very next night.

"Hello Isobel," that's what he calls me. "You know I won and I won big!" He was thrilled to be following in his father's footsteps politically. I just grinned and thought about his big feet. Adam the IVth, is in the New York State Assembly, and has already been reelected.

The ink on our divorce papers was barely dry when Adam married Hazel. After their marriage, Adam wanted Maude to kind of hang around and be friendly with his new wife. But Hazel was the snobby type who thought she was too good for regular people like Maude. There were a lot of people who didn't like her. Maude was a devoted friend of mine and she refused to be Hazel's buddy. After Adam mistreated her, then Hazel had a change of heart and became real nice all of a sudden. She wanted someone to tell her troubles to. She ran to Maude. Hazel Scott never imagined in her wildest dreams that she and Adam would ever be divorced, that one day she would have to marry another man, and that man would mistreat her, and then she would up and die.

At my age now, I see things so differently. If it hadn't been for my sister, I probably would have still been with Adam. What other woman had as much as I had? And was treated like I was treated? I may not have stayed with him, but I would not have divorced him.

Like Edward VIII, who gave up his throne for Wallis Simpson, Adam was willing to give up everything he had for me. Ms. Simpson was not royalty, had been divorced, and was actually married when she met the Prince. In order to marry her, Edward was forced to abdicate his throne. Similar to Ms. Simpson, I had been a showgirl, was a divorcee, and had a child. Adam would have given up everything for me. He didn't make that sacrifice for anyone else. Even when his father threatened to disinherit him, he stood tall and told his father, "I'm a man! I don't need anything you've got!" What difference does it make that I didn't go to finishing school or that my father wasn't a doctor. Adam loved me and I loved him. Adam was good to me! That's all I can say. He was the most considerate husband a woman could have.

When Adam came to family gatherings with me, all the young people would be so excited. They wanted to know what he was doing now and what famous person he had met recently or who had come by the apartment. Years ago I had initiated family gatherings before family reunions became popular. Everyone would bring something and we'd try to have it at a different house. We even let Maude come after a while. I just thought it was important for the family to get together and for the little ones to know who everybody else was. Now I can barely make it to my own house. But I have the memories and the pictures, so many pictures.

I go up to the island every summer now. Generally I arrive the last part of June and stay through September, though for the last year or two, I've been staying until October. It's beautiful on the island then and there aren't so many people. We have a fishing girdy on the island in the fall. All the fishermen come. It's a different group of people all together that attend because most of the people who summer at the island have gone home by that time.

I spend my mornings at my desk writing. At the far left of the room is the large black fishing net draped on the wall with various shells. Adam used to lay it in the water and pull it in to catch the little tiny fish that we would use for bait. The outriggers from our boat are also there. And right over my desk are all the fishing rods that Adam and I fished with. In that room, I haven't changed a thing. It's just like Adam left it.

I still invite guests up and entertain in Oak Bluffs, just not as often as before because I do get tired. And from time to time, I still make my famous Bloody Marys. I've been told they are the best this side of heaven. What I love to do is sit on my porch, greet the neighbors who walk by, and think about old times. Even though I think about the past, I like to surround myself with younger people because they keep me young. I still keep my nose in the paper because I want to know what's going on. And I'm still working out one political move.

Adam brought some of his politicking up here to Oak Bluffs and got the road in front of our house paved. We usually came up by train, but the chauffeur would meet us here and we'd use the car from time to time to run errands. A paved road was much appreciated by most of the residents. Now, the street on the corner is named for Dorothy West. I think it should be named for Adam and will keep petitioning these folks to make this change. Either they will change the street name because they're tired of hearing from me, or they'll stop hearing from me because I'm no longer here.

We used to go crabbing or clamming and I'd fix my famous New England Clam Chowder soup. Adam and his father taught me all about the tides. The crabs leave the lake to go out into the sound on an outgoing tide and then, on the incoming tide, they come back through the ponds where they live. So in order to catch them, you really have to get the tides right. Most of these people who come over now don't know nothing about tides. They just go down there and if there are any babies floating around they grab them and they die. They don't grow. This is how you lose what you have. There's over-crabbing. You still don't need a license to go crabbing but you do need a license to clam. The people who clam know that.

At the end of a day of fishing, entertaining, and cocktailing, Adam and I would climb the stairs to the bedroom, the wood groaning under his weight. I want the world to know that he was the perfect husband, lover and friend. I have always loved him. The first time I voted it was in Harlem with Adam. My first exposure to voting was through him. He is my number one candidate. He knows that I am *his* Belle, ringing for him forever. Once in bed, we would say to each other "Good night Bunny."

Adam was one man who did the job of a hundred. I never found another Adam, but one of these young people walking around might be the next Adam. One of the special education children that I took an interest in could be the next Adam. That's one of the reasons I dedicate so much of my time to the youth. I want them to know that they can make a difference, each and every one of them. Without young people there is no future because us old folks won't be here much longer.

I haven't fished in I don't know how long but I'm a great fisherwoman. I have Adam and Old Man Powell to thank for that. Of course, now somebody else had to put the bait worms on the hook and take the fish off the line. My job was to catch fish and I could do that very well. After catching and cleaning fish, sometimes I bake it, but I really like to fry it in a little corn meal. I'm never without collard greens and I like my rice. And I've just gotten so that I can eat broccoli again. I like my food nice and hot with plenty of hot sauce. I even call myself a spice girl. And after I've eaten , I have some sherbert to cool my mouth off. I've been trying to tell this story for a very long time and now that I've told it, my tongue is burning. I need to go have some sherbert to cool my mouth off.

Epilogue

On May 1st, 2007, Harlem lost its queen. Isabel lay in bed heavily medicated but there was no comfort in the sheets. The loved ones surrounding her bed hung onto each breath as her chest rose and fell. But even they were surprised when Isabel sat up and turned her legs to the side of the bed as though she might actually get up.

"My son is here!" she said, with a tone of pride smothered in motherly love as Preston walked into the room.

"Are you hungry?" she asked, pushing back the tug of death for a moment so she could greet her only child one last time. She fell back into her semi-comatose state and a few moments later she left us to be reunited with her beloved Bunny Boy. She reclaimed her role as Adam's Belle. That fourth-floor corner of St. Nicholas Avenue in Harlem will never ever be the same without the fiery little lady who touched and brightened up so many lives.

Isabel Washington Powell lived to see her memoir completed but sadly passed away before its publication. God blessed us with her presence for nearly a century. It was truly a one hundred year celebration of life. One of her favorite sayings was, "If I should die right now, don't cry for me... I've had a wonderful life, baby!"

A memorial service was held on May 12, 2007 at Abyssinian Baptist Church. The Reverend Calvin Butts presided over the service. Belle's ashes were scattered at Martha's Vineyard.

ADAM CLAYTON POWELL, IV
68ᵀᴴ Assembly District

New York County

THE ASSEMBLY

STATE OF NEW YORK

ALBANY

CHAIRMAN
Subcommittee on Insurer Investments
Market Practices in Underserved Are

COMMITTEES
Corporations, Authorities
and Commissions
Housing
Insurance
Small Business

MEMBER
The New York State
Black, Puerto Rican, Hispanic
and Asian Legislative Caucus

May 11, 2007

To the family and friends of Isabelle Powell:

I was deeply saddened to hear of the passing of Isabelle. We met some twenty years ago. I always felt a special closeness to her and she treated me like family as well. She was my father's first love and I can certainly see why. She was a wonderful and lovely lady who enjoyed life to the fullest. Her charm, her grace and her beauty were evident no matter what.

I still have fond memories of visiting her in Martha's Vineyard a few years ago. The late Ethel Kennedy had invited me to the Kennedy compound for a clambake. But rather than drive, I decided to cruise for three days on my boat so I could stopover in Martha's Vineyard and surprise Isabelle. Every summer she would invite me and I figured this was the perfect opportunity to go. So I called her from the boat and asked if we could come by. "Of course!" she said happily surprised and as soon as I got to the house she had a Bloody Mary waiting for me. I loved it! Visiting her in the house she and my dad shared in the 1930s was the highlight of my 5-day voyage. I remember her showing me my dad's fishing rods still on display on the wall….and good enough for another fishing trip. We had a great day!

We know that you are in better hands but we will miss you "Belle"……until we meet again.

Keeping the Faith,

Adam Clayton Powell, IV
Member of Assembly
68th District

Email Address: powella@assembly.state.ny.us
❑ ALBANY OFFICE: Room 527, Legislative Office Building, Albany, New York 12248, (518) 455-4781
❑ DISTRICT OFFICE: 87 East 116ᵀᴴ Street, New York, New York 10029, (212) 828-3953
♻ Printed on recycled paper.

Barack Obama

May 12, 2007

Dear Friends,

Isabel Powell was a woman of great strength and compassion who believed, as she put it, that "Life is precious and it should be enjoyed." Her loss is felt deeply by her family and many friends, from Abyssinian Baptist Church and the rest of New York City to Martha's Vineyard and beyond.

Mrs. Powell was a partner to Adam Clayton Powell as he helped lay the foundations that have made my career possible, but she was much more than that. Isabel Washington was always an independent woman. From her career as a well-known Broadway actress to teacher and matriarch of the Powell family, she brought an infectious energy to everything she did.

Michelle and I are saddened by Isabel Powell's passing and our hearts go out to her family and all of you gathered here today.

Sincerely,

Barack Obama

WILLIAM JEFFERSON CLINTON

May 9, 2007

To the Family and Friends of Isabel Powell:

I was deeply saddened by Isabel's death, and I
extend my heartfelt sympathy to everyone
gathered today to celebrate her good life.

Isabel was a remarkable woman. In 30 years as
a special education teacher and a lifetime as
an advocate for the youth of Harlem, she
continually pushed the boundaries that society
imposed upon her community and inspired
generations of young people to do the same.
She has raised the hopes and dreams of
countless individuals, and in so doing, has
built a brighter future for us all.

While Isabel's achievements as a public servant
are well noted, her charm and grace are equally
legendary. Her warmth of character and
compassion for others shone through to any who
met her, and visitors to her home enjoyed a
sincere and often unforgettable conversation,
served with an equally memorable pot of her
famous chili.

We will all miss her, but Hillary and I hope
that her friends and family are comforted by
the knowledge that she left this world a better
place than she found it.

Sincerely,

Bill Clinton

Index

About the Authors

As a native of Los Angeles, California, Joyce Burnett has always been interested in music, entertainment and fitness. She knew little, however, about the dynamic sounds and lifestyle of the Harlem Renaissance until she ran head on into Isabel Washington Powell, the glamorous showgirl from the 1920's who married the late Congressman Adam Clayton Powell, Jr. From the moment they met, Joyce was enthralled by the vivid pictures Belle painted of her life.

The motivating factor for Joyce in writing this book was that Belle's story absolutely had to be included in the historical record. Belle reminded Joyce of her own Aunt Ceola. She dressed impeccably, cooked better than most chefs, and approached situations with a touch of sass. Belle's life was truly fantastic and it was the best story that had never been told.

Joyce began this project shortly after publishing an article on her experience as a Peace Corps volunteer in the Islamic Republic of Mauritania. She worked closely with Belle for almost ten years to record this incredible story. Belle was very pleased with the early draft of Adam's Belle, but sadly, she passed away before her story was published.

Joyce holds degrees from Wesleyan University, Johns Hopkins, and American University. She remains an avid fitness enthusiast.